Lt 282.092 Noo
Noonan, Peggy, 1950-
John Paul the Great :
remembering a spiritual father /

34028062492765
CY $14.95 ocm76876754

3 4028 06249 2765
HARRIS COUNTY PUBLIC LIBRARY

JAN − − 2007

JOHN PAUL THE GREAT

WITHDRAWN
PRINT

WITHDRAWN
PRINT

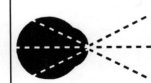

This Large Print Book carries the
Seal of Approval of N.A.V.H.

JOHN PAUL THE GREAT
REMEMBERING A SPIRITUAL FATHER

PEGGY NOONAN

LARGE PRINT PRESS
An imprint of Thomson Gale, a part of The Thomson Corporation

Detroit • New York • San Francisco • New Haven, Conn. • Waterville, Maine • London

Copyright © 2005 by Peggy Noonan

Thomson Gale is part of The Thomson Corporation.

Thomson and Star Logo and Large Print Press are trademarks and Gale is a registered trademark used herein under license.

ALL RIGHTS RESERVED
The text of this Large Print edition is unabridged.
Other aspects of the book may vary from the original edition.
Set in 16 pt. Plantin.

LIBRARY OF CONGRESS CATALOGING-IN-PUBLICATION DATA

Noonan, Peggy, 1950-
  John Paul the Great : remembering a spiritual father / by Peggy Noonan.
  — Large print ed.
    p. cm. — (Thorndike Press large print core)
  ISBN 1-59722-129-5 (lg. print : hc : alk. paper)
  ISBN 1-59413-156-2 (lg. print : sc : alk. paper)
  1. John Paul II, Pope, 1920- 2. Popes — Biography. 3. Large type books. I. Title.
BX1378.5.N64 2005
282.092—dc22   2005026138

ISBN 13: 978-1-59413-156-1
Published in 2006 by arrangement with Viking Penguin,
a member of Penguin Group (USA) Inc.

Printed in the United States of America on permanent paper
10 9 8 7 6 5 4 3 2 1

For Bently Elliot
and Michael Novak

ACKNOWLEDGMENTS

All books are brought into being by little platoons. I thank my son Will for his patience, and my friends Stephanie and Ransom Wilson, Tom Clancy, Bill Sykes, Marie Brenner and Ben Elliott for their encouragement. Thanks also go to Michael Novak and Father Richard John Neuhaus, for their inspiring words and writings.

My friend Joni Evans, whom I met when she helped edit my first book, is everything one wants in a literary agent (insightful, honest, stalwart) and needs in a friend. I am deeply grateful to her.

At Viking Penguin I thank Susan Petersen Kennedy, Clare Ferraro, Pam Dorman, and Rick Kot. I sometimes worked on this book at Armando's restaurant in Brooklyn; I thank its owner and staff for their graciousness and good cheer.

CONTENTS

FOREWORD

Some historical events are spiritual events. One that was both led to this book.

In the days and months after 9/11/01 something beautiful happened in America. The event seemed to deepen us. We had up to that point as a nation been on quite a tear — of materialism, of carelessness. But then the shock came, and the grief, and a national sense of being violated and brought down. And in that terrible gravity — in the falling of the buildings, if you will — a liberation of sorts occurred.

If you were in New York that day you remember that the terrible fall of the buildings created a rush of air upwards. It sent paper in the air, it whooshed thousands of pounds of paper into the air so that people's business cards and wills and employment data wound up scattered all over within a radius of miles.

The great fall unleashed some things and pushed them up. And in my mind or imagination that upward force helped disperse a new and beautiful liberation as to faith and religion, of love of country and love of our fellowman. I remember the little religious shrines that popped up all over Manhattan. I remember the air of reverence. It seemed an appropriate response to what we then knew was the beginning of difficult times. We had entered the age of terror. Now we know what time it is.

In the years since, that spirit has lessened, but it has not gone away. It will come up again when we have bad times again.

As for me, after 9/11 my own thoughts were in a way liberated. My subject matter changed, turning more toward my faith, and I found myself more and more looking toward Rome, and the great old man who lived there until the past year. I found myself writing about him in the *Wall Street Journal* and elsewhere with a new question in mind: Why do those of us who love him love him? How to explain it to those who did not or could not?

And so this book, a remembrance of John Paul II, and an attempt to capture some of his greatness. It is written with the conviction that the great deserve our loyalty and that those who have added to life, who have inspired the living and pointed to a better way, should be learned from and lauded.

CHAPTER ONE

I Saw a Saint at Sunset

It was early morning in the Vatican, July 2, 2003, a brilliant morning in the middle of the worst Roman heat wave in a century. The city was quiet, the streets soft with the heat. It was the summer of the dress code battle between the tourists and the guards at St. Peter's Basilica. The tourists wanted to wear shorts and halter tops; this was in violation of the Vatican dress code (slacks, shirts with sleeves), and the guards wouldn't let them in. There were arguments at the entrance, and angry words. Soon a Roman compromise was achieved: No one lost face; everyone got what they needed. The vendors in St. Peter's Square were allowed to sell paper shirts and pants for a euro apiece. The tourists would put them on over their clothes, walk past the guards, and tear the paper off as they entered the dark cool of the church.

By 7:45 a.m., hundreds of us had gathered in the Piazza del Sant'Uffizio, in the shadow of Bernini's colonnade, the marble columns that curve outward to embrace St. Peter's Square. Already the heat was gathering, and we fanned ourselves with thin green papal audience tickets. The crowd was happy — chirping nuns, clicking tourists. We were about to see the pope. We were about to see John Paul.

We are a mix of tourists, the curious, and the faithful: a group of deaf Italian adults in white baseball caps, with silk Vatican flags tied around their necks; members of a choir from the Archdiocese of St. Louis, Missouri; a group of nuns from the Little Mission for the Deaf in Bologna. There was a man from Monterrey, Mexico, with his wife and two children. As the crowd grew, we were pressed so close I could smell the spray starch on his green cotton shirt.

"Why are you here?" I asked.

"To see the pope," he said. "He is the most important Christian in the world. He is the follower of Christ." When, a few minutes later, I read the quote back to him from my notebook, he edited it. "He is the most important *person* in the whole world."

I talked to a woman in a hat made of hay. Spiky yellow straw, actually, the brim down to shade her face. She was forty-five or fifty years old and looked like pictures of the older, weathered Greta Garbo. She told me she was on a pilgrimage. She had walked hundreds of kilometers in a circuitous tour of Marian sites. She and her husband — bearish, gray bearded — had departed upper Austria in May and had arrived here yesterday, on July 1st. They had walked on highways and small roads. She showed me her diary of the pilgrimage: In neat precise script she had documented every church they had seen along the way. Her husband had drawn pictures of cathedrals in blue ballpoint ink. He had taken snapshots of little chapels and pasted them in the diary. "Here," she said to me, indicating a page on which she had made comic line drawings. They showed angular feet bruised by exaggerated calluses. Next to them she had drawn the lotions and bandages she had put upon her wounds. They had gone to mass every day of their six-week journey, she said.

Why had they come here?

"Why? To see Il Papa!" She gestured as if to say: *This is the culmination.*

We filed through metal detectors that did not seem to work, no beeping or bopping, no one watching things closely. It is surprising to see metal detectors here, for a crowd like this, but the last time someone planned to kill the pope, in the Philippines, the would-be assassin meant to dress as a priest. Soon we were directed through a paved area just off St. Peter's Square. (Later, when I would return to it, a young priest would tell me, "We think he may have been crucified under here." I shook my head. "Saint Peter. It may have been just about here, down there." And he pointed at the pavement.)

We entered the Paul VI Audience Hall, an enormous concrete structure, cavernous and modern, like a big suburban church, or an evangelical McChurch at the edge of a city. Rows of fixed seats were aligned toward the stage. People were coming in single file and in groups, hundreds of them and then thousands. As I walked among them, I heard the languages of France, England, Mexico, Austria, the Czech Republic. There were groups from West Africa, Germany, Poland, Scotland, Portugal, and Brazil. A Romanian chorus of middle-aged women began to sing softly in their seats. When they finished, a choir from Bialystok, Poland, thirty young women and men, began to sing lustily.

16

Suddenly a rustling up front. Dozens of tall African women danced in, laughing and clapping in floor-length white cotton dresses. On the hems were sewn the words "Archdiocese of Freetown," in Sierra Leone. They sat next to Catholic school-children from Rwanda, who were clapping and shaking tambourines.

I thought: *The whole church is here.*

The room rocked. Cheering here, drums there, an American spiritual crooned somewhere in the back. The choruses would pick up one another's sound, so that a group from Santo Domingo would sing, and as they finished, a young male choir from Poland, in white tie and tails, would take up the song. Then as they finished, a group of Indians of the Americas, in native dress and full headdresses — they looked like beautiful peacocks — would beat native drums. It was as if the disparate but unified members of the audience, as they echoed and supported one another, were a living symbol of the church every day in the world.

And now something came alive on the stage. Two Swiss Guards in their purple and orange uniforms, big red plumes on their black helmets, entered the stage and stood erect in the middle, with halberds. Then a flurry of cardinals and bishops in black, with red and purple sashes. Then two papal chamberlains in white tie and tails.

We looked to the left of the stage. There was movement.

It was him, the pope — twenty minutes early. The woman next to me, a regular audiencegoer, laughed. "When he's ready, he's ready these days," she yelled to me over the noise.

John Paul was rolled slowly onto the stage. He was seated in a brown wooden chair that rested within a kind of wooden rig on little wheels. It was like a wheel-throne; it was like the kind of big wooden roller they use to get something off the top shelf at Home Depot. It looked both practical and absurd.

Everyone applauded, and as I clapped, I looked around me and saw faces set in a determinedly pleasant look, as if they were thinking, *I am so happy to see you, but the sight of you is breaking my heart.*

He was dressed all in white, bent forward in his chair. White surplice, white zucchetto — the skullcap popes wear — white gold-fringed sash. As the wheel-throne reached the center of the stage the pope was surrounded by a scrum of aides and cardinals. They helped him to his feet, helped transfer him to a white upholstered high-backed chair. Then they turned it toward us.

He looked out at us. We looked back at him. His face was — oh, his face!

I thought of the girl on his last trip to Canada, a year before. She was a child, six or so, and she had it in her head that the pope was the best person in the world. So her parents brought her to a big outdoor Mass, and she was chosen to give him flowers. She walked up to him with her little bouquet and held it toward him. He leaned his upper body toward her in his chair. Then she turned and ran sobbing from the stage with what seemed like panic. Because he was old and his head was big and his neck and back were curled, and the effort to lift his head so you could see his face drew his features down, and the parkinsonian mask that froze his face made him look angry, or ill-meaning, or sad. The poor child ran.

Now the crowd took to its feet and the applause was continuous. But it was also muted, not full of joy as the crowd had been before the audience had begun.

His cassock was too short — six inches off the floor. We could see his white cotton sports socks. We could see his worn brown shoes! He wears old loafers, like a workingman, and not the traditional dainty slippers of a pope.

"We love you, Papa!" someone called out. "We love you, Holy Father."

He lifted his head with effort. We took our seats. Suddenly I realized the purpose of a Vatican announcement that had been issued the week before. The Holy Father, the press office said, would not go hiking in the hills this summer as he had in the past, but instead would work through his vacation writing a memoir of his early years as priest and bishop. Tourists buzzed about this: How amazing that the old man would produce a book on his time off! What they didn't notice, what had been cleverly obscured by the announcement, was that the pope's legs don't work anymore. Of course he wasn't hiking.

When I mentioned this later to a priest in Rome, he laughed. John Paul, he said, has grown sensitive about speculation regarding his illnesses and had recently groused, half comically, to an American cardinal, "Tell those American journalists the pope doesn't run the church with his feet."

The pope read to us from remarks typed on white letter-sized paper. His voice was blurry and thick. The papers trembled in his hand. He spoke in Italian. The thin-neck microphone into which he spoke was sensitive; we could hear him breathe between the sentences. People in the audience became distracted. Then the pope spoke in Polish and his voice became stronger, and even though most of the people in the audience didn't understand what he was saying, they quieted, and leaned forward.

He had a pronounced tremor in his left arm, and during the translation he leaned his head and rested his chin on his left hand, to stop the shaking. Then he cleared his throat and spoke in English. But the only words I could make out were "the spirit of the Beatitudes." Later I read the Associated Press report of the pope's message. He had spoken of Psalm 145, which he called "a song of praise for the morning." It ends, he said, "in a proclamation of the sovereignty of God over human history." It reminds us, he said, that "the Lord shall reign forever."

Schoolchildren from Santo Domingo

cheered the old chant: *Juan Pablo Segundo, te quiere todo el mundo.*

He raised his right hand to acknowledge the chants. The playfulness of the past — the way he used to wave with both hands, up and down, and say "Woo woo!" to the children who cheered him in New York and Chicago so long ago — was not possible for him anymore.

And yet as I watched him, I realized I did not see him as ill and frail. I saw him as encased — trapped in there, in an outer immobility. Outside he is old and frail, but inside he is John Paul, the one who had walked out on the Vatican balcony and dazzled the crowd twenty-four years before. And for the first time I thought: *He is a victim soul.* His suffering has meaning, it is telling us something. He is giving us something, a parting gift.

He sang to us a little at the end, like an old man sitting in the sun. Most of us couldn't tell the words or the tune, but he was doing it for us, and there was something so beautiful and moving in it. I turned to a friend. "We are hearing a saint singing," I said. I wanted to put my hands over my ears so I could hold the sound in my head forever.

★ ★ ★

Throughout all this I would look over now and then at a young woman, a red-haired girl sitting with a Polish choir. She was nineteen or twenty, clean faced, pale. From the moment the pope had entered the room she had not taken her eyes off him. And she had not stopped weeping.

Now John Paul made the sign of the cross. The cardinals came and knelt before him and kissed his hand. The Indians of the Americas mounted the stage to kneel before him. Dozens of newlywed couples in gowns and tuxedos mounted the stage two by two to receive his blessing. Then the sick — children rolled out onto the stage in hospital beds, people in wheel-chairs.

I always got the feeling with John Paul that if he could have narrowed down the people he met and blessed to those he loved most, they would not be cardinals, princes, or congressmen, but nuns from obscure convents and Down syndrome children, especially the latter. Because they have suffered, and because in some serious and amazing way the love of God seems more immediately available to them. Ev-eryone else gets themselves tied up in am-

23

bition and ideas and bustle, all the great distractions, but the modest and unwell are so often unusually open to this message: God loves us, his love is all around us, he made us to love him and be happy.

A friend of mine who used to work with retarded children told me once that Down syndrome children would often ask her to comb her long blond hair. She'd take it out of its ponytail, give it a shake, and they'd run in it. They'd touch it and pat it and walk through it as they would curtains. It takes a kind of spiritual genius to know a hunk of hair is heaven. They knew. The pope knows they know.

And then the audience was over. The handlers and cardinals descended again, surrounded the pope, hauled him up, and helped him transfer from the white chair back to the wheel-throne. They began to push him from the stage.

He turned to us, raised his right hand, and made a halting sign of the cross. And then the Poles in the audience broke into the song that went back to the beginning, the authentic sound of twenty-three years earlier, when John Paul first walked onto the Vatican balcony and looked out at the world. They had sung it for him at every stop along the way of his long papacy, through good times and bad. "*Sto lat, Sto lat,* May you live a hundred years."

I stayed until the very end, two hours. Then I turned around to look at all the people standing behind me, to see their faces so I could describe them in this book. And I was taken aback, because they were gone. Two thirds of the audience had already left, had gone before the pope had even departed the stage. As if they'd had their tickets punched — *I saw the old guy* — and were on their way next to see the cats in the Colosseum. The only ones who remained were the ones who would not, could not, go, like the Polish girl who sat and wept.

His whole life was a good-bye tour now. He knew they came to see him in part because they wanted to be able to say, "I saw John Paul the Great." And so there was at all these events, and around him, a sense of inescapable twilight.

An explosion of sadness would mark his passing. Yes, it was time for a new man, one who hadn't been so battered by history. But John Paul was a giant, the last pope of the old age. After him the real modern world would begin, the new one, the post-9/11 one, and much would be in play. His presence was as weighty and dense as the old Vatican itself, and his departure would seem to leave a void in the landscape.

His suffering was his witness. Every other leader in the world stands straight and tall; they employ scores of aides who tell them to throw back their shoulders and walk forward looking like the leader of France, or England, or America. These public souls are acutely conscious of their public presentation. But John Paul came out broken and bent, as broken as the Christ on the cross he carried on his crozier.

When asked how he was, he often joked, "I'm in good shape from the neck up! Not so good from the neck down."

An aide who had watched him for a long time asked him once, "Do you ever cry?"

"Not outside," he replied.

When I returned from Rome, I talked to the writer Michael Novak about the meaning of the suffering of the pope. He spoke of Saint Thérèse of Lisieux, who believed her suffering could be given by her, could be almost lifted out of her, to help others. She would take her moments of pain or sadness and offer them to God, believing they could in this way become united with his great love, united, that is, with an infinitely powerful force. She would ask that her suffering be used to help the missionaries of the world, that her pain be used to make their day sweeter, their efforts more fruitful. She knew, Michael said, what Dostoyevsky knew: There's a kind of web around the world, an electric web in which we're all united, all connected in suffering and in love. When you add to it what you have, you add to the circuitry of love.

Thérèse was a Carmelite, and Michael spoke of the papal biographer George Weigel's observation that John Paul II had a Carmelite soul, a soul at home with the tradition of everyday mysticism. That tradition is informed by a conviction that all is connected, all is part of a wholeness.

The pope's suffering tells us, Michael said, that it is important in an age like ours to look beyond the surficial. We honor and adore surface things — beauty, youth, grace, vigor. And it's understandable: They're beautiful. But the pope reminds us it is crucial to see the beauty in the old, the infirm, the imperfect. They have a place in life, a purpose, a deep legitimacy and due.

John Paul not only said this, of course, he also lived it. He showed us this truth by presenting himself to the world each day as he was.

I found myself thinking about this lesson in the months after I'd seen the pope, but I thought he was also telling us something else. When you witnessed his fragility, you felt prompted somehow, even if it wasn't quite conscious, to recognize, and love, the fragility of all our lives. That fragility is at the heart of things, is all part of the mystery, and it finally left me thinking, every time I saw him on TV or in a picture, of the words of Dennis Potter, the great writer of television dramas, who told BBC correspondent Melvyn Bragg in a celebrated 1994 interview what it was like to die. When you are dying, he said, you look out the window and see a flowering blossom and suddenly realize how beautiful it is, how extraordinary, "the whitest, frothiest, blossomest blossom that there ever could be."

By dying in public the old pope got us thinking about dying, which got us thinking about living, and life. And maybe feeling more tenderly toward it.

When he died I think we got a clue as to how much it all cost him, and what he felt.

He asked, in his final requests, that a square of white silk be placed over his face in his casket. No one in the Vatican explained why. Then they announced it was "a new ritual." John Paul, in his papers, did not explain the request.

He did refer, however, in the last years of his papacy, to how he experienced life each day. Repeatedly pressed to retire, to give himself some rest after his mighty labors, he refused. "Christ didn't come down from the cross," he said.

But here's a funny thing: When I think of him now, I do not see him as he was last year or five years ago or even a decade ago. I do not see him as the John Paul I met, and whose hand I kissed. I see him as he was. I see him in my mind's eye as the man who walked out on the Vatican loggia one night in 1978, at dusk, when the sight of him was another kind of shock, and when his astounding papacy began.

CHAPTER TWO

Wake Up, a Pope Is Coming

Do you know what a lion he was? And what it was first like to see him? It was autumn 1978, in the earliest part of the Roman evening, the huge lights of the television networks hurriedly trained on the Vatican balcony as a stranger walked out. What a lion he was, and for all his loving tones, what a roar.

John Paul. Joannes Paulus. Giovanni Paolo II. Bishop of Rome, Vicar of Christ, Successor to Peter, Supreme Pontiff, Servant of the Servants of God, Holy Father. One of the longest-serving popes in history, whose papacy will be judged by history as bigger than all but a score of the 263 pontiffs before him.

Somehow, and it wasn't only a matter of his relative youthfulness, those who were there when he became pope knew he would be with us for a long time. When he went to kiss the new pope's ring moments after John Paul II had been elected, his Polish colleague and occasional antagonist, Cardinal Stefan Wyszynski, said, "You will take the church into the third millennium." Then Wyszynski attempted to kneel. John Paul wouldn't let him, lifting him and embracing him instead.

It was October 1978, at the end of the year of the three popes. What an amazing time.

First, Pope Paul VI died. He had been pope from June 21, 1963 until August 6, 1978, a fifteen-year reign. At the end, as his life was leaving him — he'd had a heart attack at the papal summer home, Castel Gandolfo, in the hills beyond Rome — he made confession, took communion, and spoke his last words, the Lord's Prayer. He was eighty years old and perhaps not so sad to die. His weariness, at the end, is reflected in his most famous comment, that "in youth the days are short and the years are long. In old age the years are short and the days are long." He struggled to guide the church into modernity, and he had followed a tough act: John XXIII, the kindly old pope who'd called and created the Second Vatican Council, burst through a carrying wall of church history, and captured the affection of the world. To Paul would fall the hard work of imposing and implementing the myriad decisions, directives, and suggestions of what came to be known as Vatican II.

Paul VI was mourned, summed up, and buried. He was followed in quick order by John Paul I, "the pope of the half-moon," who was elected to the papacy by the College of Cardinals on August 26, 1978. Cardinal Albino Luciani, the archbishop of Venice, had taken for himself the name John Paul I in a nod of fidelity and loyalty to his predecessors, the happy pope and the sadder one.

Cardinal Luciani was the Last of the Acceptable Italians. For 456 years the cardinals of the church had been picking Italian popes, and tradition in the Vatican is hard to shake. But in the 1970s, the Italian cardinals were split left, right, and center over Vatican II, over how its reforms should be understood and implemented. Cardinal Luciani was seen neither as a "liberal" nor as a "conservative" (I use quotes here because in terms of modern Catholic doctrine and teaching — not to mention practice, local variations, and statements on political and economic matters — the meaning of these terms can be maddeningly murky) and was elected quickly.

There had been some talk, in the conclave that had made Cardinal Luciani John

Paul I, of Karol Wojtyla, the brilliant young cardinal from Kraków, Poland. An American reporter had bumped into Cardinal Wojtyla in the Vatican Gardens just before the voting began, and asked him: Do you think it possible you will be chosen pope? The Polish cardinal smiled, shook his head, and replied in English. "I am not *papabile,*" he said. I am not a possible pope.

In retrospect, it was reminiscent of what he had said forty years before, when a high school friend asked him if he was thinking of becoming a priest. "I am not worthy," he had replied.

The new pope, John Paul I, had apparently not wanted the papacy, but had accepted it. He told friends he was not sure he possessed the physical strength necessary to withstand the pressures of the job. He was a man of considerable humility and sweetness — his father, a migrant worker, had been a Socialist Party organizer, and when he himself was a cardinal, he had sold the golden pectoral cross he wore on his chest to raise money for the needy — and his fellow cardinals were drawn to his personality and character. They were pleased, too, by this: After the dour and pale Paul VI, Cardinal Luciani was a man who could encounter the world with a look of pleasure on his face, with a smile.

So the College of Cardinals elected him, disbanded, and everyone went home.

John Paul I was just beginning to make a broadly favorable impression when on the thirty-fourth day of his papacy, early in the morning, a nun went into the papal apartment to wake him and found him dead in bed, turned on his side, the reading light still on, papers spread around him. He had died of what appeared to be a massive heart attack. He was still wearing his reading glasses.

The world was shocked. Popes reigned for decades, not weeks. Soon and perhaps inevitably came rumors of foul play. *He must have been killed in his bed. Maybe they suffocated him with a pillow. No, it was poison. They did it because he wanted to clean up the Vatican bank. No, it was because he wanted to reorganize the Curia, so they reorganized him first.*

The rumors were fueled when it became clear the Vatican had attempted a cover-up of a small detail. A church official had decided it should not become known that it was a woman, a nun, who had found the pope dead in bed. This, even though the papal apartments had long been tended by nuns. The Vatican secretary of state, Cardinal Jean Villot, accordingly changed the first official announcements to insist the pope's body had been discovered by John Paul's male secretary, Monsignor John Magee.

Two generations of investigative journalists and historians have gone after the story, and not one has come up with evidence supporting the murder theory. And yet the death of John Paul I endures to a degree as a mystery, mostly because of the simple fact of it. How could something so astounding happen?

Maybe some of the answer is suggested by a scene in Carl Bernstein and Marco Politi's book on John Paul II, *His Holiness.* They recount a dinner that took place a few nights before John Paul I died. He was dining with Cardinal Jean Villot. John Paul is quoted as telling his secretary of state, "Another man better than I could have been chosen [pope]. Paul VI already pointed out his successor. He was sitting just in front of me in the Sistine Chapel." He was referring to Cardinal Wojtyla of Poland. "He will come because I will go,"

John Paul I prophesied.

Many years later Monsignor Magee would tell this story. When asked what name he would take as pope, Cardinal Luciani answered, "John Paul the first." When told he could not be called the first until there was a second, Luciani replied, "He will come soon enough."

Here is another intriguing story, this one from *New York Times* reporter Tad Szulc's biography of John Paul II. It, too, suggests a certain element of destiny.

The elderly Pope Paul VI had known young Cardinal Wojtyla well and had favored him with important appointments, working with him on the preparation of some of the documents of Vatican II. In this way, Cardinal Wojtyla was given the opportunity not only to do significant and important work, but also to meet most of the movers and shakers of the church. Szulc reports that Paul VI had wanted Karol Wojtyla to be the first non-Italian pope, and that Cardinal Wojtyla knew this.

A strange thing happened when Pope Paul died. Years before, when he was a young man, Paul, then a young priest named Giovanni Battista Montini, was given his first big assignment as the Vatican's representative in Warsaw. (Paul was ordained eleven days after Karol Wojtyla's birth, and went to Warsaw when Karol was three years old.) Father Montini came to have a special love for Poland, to appreciate its mysticism and respect its literature. This may be in part why, years later, he was so alert to and sensitive to the particular gifts of the young cardinal from Kraków.

While he was living in Warsaw, young Father Montini saw in a small store an alarm clock that particularly pleased him. He bought it and kept it by his bed for the rest of his life.

That old clock was at his bedside when Pope Paul died. At the moment he expired, for no apparent reason, the Polish alarm clock, which had not been set to go off, began to ring loudly, as if it were announcing something. As if it were saying, "A Pole is coming; a new day is about to begin."

This story is not spoken of much but has been noted by many of John Paul's biographers. The seemingly unexplainable aspect of it, the perhaps supernatural aspect, seems to have been lost on none of them.

So now John Paul I, "the pope of the half-moon," was dead, and the cardinals of the church had to gather once again to choose a new one. The phrase "of the half-moon" is Saint Malachi's, considered by the somewhat superstitious, the mystically inclined, and those with perhaps too much time on their hands to have been a saint with a great and specific gift of prophecy. Malachi was a twelfth-century Irish priest who, while visiting Rome, had a startling series of visions, the facts of which he wrote down. In the visions he was told of every pope who would follow the pope of the time, Celestine II, who died in 1144. Each of the 112 successive popes was fore-told to Malachi, who summed up each man with a three- or four-word phrase. John Paul I was called "of the half-moon." And in fact, he was pope from one half-moon to the next.

The official church position is that the prophecies of Malachi, discovered in Vatican archives three hundred years ago, may be a forgery. But the power of the prophecies endures among some of the rank and file, in large part because Malachi's descriptions of each of the popes for the past three hundred years has seemed prescient to some degree, sometimes remarkably so.

So it is interesting how Saint Malachi characterized the man who would follow the pope of the half-moon. He said it would be a man whose papacy would be captured by these words: "Of the labors of the sun." The greatest of our stars, the thing that lights and warms the world.

Over two days there were seven ballots. Each of them had been followed by black smoke issued from the chimney of the Sistine Chapel, where the cardinals met and the voting took place. It was the ancient tradition: Ballots that did not yield a pope were burned in a way that yielded black smoke; ballots that produced a pope would be burned in a way that sent white smoke wafting.

This election was a struggle, but finally the white smoke came. Dusk was falling, and the crowd in St. Peter's Square began to grow. They didn't know who the new pope was; they only knew they had one. Sophisticates and journalists stood by with lists of all the frontrunners in their hands.

Now it was nighttime, just after dusk, 7:17 p.m.; October 16, 1978.

The Swiss Guard marched into the square. The papal flag was unfurled from the central loggia of the basilica, directly above the vestibule of St. Peter's. A cardinal of the church came onto the balcony to address the crowd. It was Cardinal Pericle Felici, himself said to have been a candidate but apparently very happy to be about to announce someone else's name.

He couldn't help it, he was half shouting.

He said the words of old, in Latin. "I announce to you a great joy . . . We have a pope." "Habemus papem." Those always moving words, joyous and full of portent.

"Habemus Pahhhhh-pemmmmmm" is the way he said it. The crowd roared.

And then Cardinal Felici announced the new pope's name, again in Latin. "Carolum Sanctae Romanae Cardinalem Wojtyla . . ."

A friend of mine was there. The moment the cardinal said the name Wojtyla, what followed was not joy but confusion. The Cardinal had pronounced it "Woy-tee-wahhhhh," and members of the crowd, predominantly Italian but many others also, just looked at one another. When you hear some of the broadcast tapes of the announcement, what you hear first is one of the network correspondents and other members of the crowd saying, "Who?"

To complicate things further, the name the cardinal said sounded to some like the name of an elderly Italian cardinal who was generally thought to be senile. So part of the muted reaction was due to the fact that some people were thinking, "The Vatican has finally gone mad."

Now there was new movement on the balcony. A sturdy, round-faced man dressed in white came forward, and smiled.

The crowd looked up and people pointed, and now they began to applaud.

You have to be older than about thirty years of age to remember when we first saw him on the central balcony of St. Peter's Basilica. The balcony faces St. Peter's Square, and on this night there were more than two hundred thousand people waiting to see the new pope. When they looked up, what they saw was startling.

He didn't look like Junior Soprano, as a number of the cardinals did, and some previous popes had. He didn't have the big glasses, or an aristocratic nose grown fleshy or a peasant's nose grown broad.

He looked Slavic. He looked young. He was a fit fifty-eight years old, the youngest pope in a century, and looked younger than his age — a solid build, straight posture, five feet eleven, and 170 pounds. Steely gray hair, deep blue eyes. He looked robust. Later it became known that he was an athlete (kayaking, biking, swimming, skiing, childhood soccer stardom). He was also, it turned out, a published poet and playwright who spoke seven languages fluently.

It was too startling to absorb at first. Word spread in the crowd, and finally was repeated on the TV networks: The new pope was the cardinal from Poland, from Kraków.

He was from the East, not the West. (But popes come from the West!) He was from the Communist bloc. (But popes come from liberal democracies!) He was from Poland. (No one comes from Poland!)

Two hundred sixty-three popes had come before him, and he was the first from that place. It seemed like a miracle whose meaning you didn't understand. And afterward the cardinals who had voted for him spoke about this, spoke of the long balloting and the struggle of the one hundred eleven cardinals to come to grips with the fact that history had taken a swerve: There were no more Italians who seemed right; it was time to have a non-Italian pope, one who was young and talented and deep in his faith, not a bureaucrat or an austere intellectual but a pope who'd had parish experience, whose career had been, essentially, to work as a priest and then a bishop with the people. Later a cardinal would tell Tad Szulc, "God forced us to break with history to elect Karol Wojtyla."

And now here he was, on the Vatican balcony, and he was radiant. You sensed it: This man is going to make it all more interesting. His home country was Communist ruled, and communism hates Catholicism. Poland's rulers had tried mightily to repress the Church or co-opt it, but Poles being Poles, it never quite worked. Instead, in Poland, the church was the great counterweight to the state, the platform from which the state could be resisted.

The crowd in St. Peter's Square didn't know what to think. The new pope seemed to understand.

In his first words to them, from the balcony, he lauded Christ and praised his predecessor, John Paul I. Then he said, "And now the most eminent cardinals have called a new bishop of Rome. They have called him from a distant country, distant but always so close through the communion in the Christian faith and tradition. . . . I do not know whether I can explain myself well in your — *our* — Italian language. If I make mistakes you will correct me! And so I present myself to you all, to confess our common faith. . . ."

It was electric. He was electric. And when they left the square that night, the two hundred thousand were not unhappy at what they had seen of this new pontiff.

Back in Poland, as word spread of what had happened, people found it impossible to believe. Word came by radio and then spread person to person, and soon half of Kraków was a candlelit street vigil. Communist Party officials found themselves moved as Poles and appalled as Communists.

In the Polish neighborhoods of America, pure joy. In Chicago, in the great Polish American parishes, people left their houses and stood in the streets. Then they went to church, and then a lot of tears were shed, and spontaneous dinners sprang up all over town. In Boston, Ray Flynn, an ambitious young politico, future mayor, and Clinton-era ambassador to the Holy See, went straight to the Polish area of South Boston, where people had just heard the news. From his memoir: "They were pouring out of their houses, wanting to share their joy, wanting to be together, wanting to celebrate. With no public square in which to congregate as they might have done back in Poland, they streamed from all directions toward the church of Our Lady of Czestochowa on Dorchester Avenue." They brought flowers. They knelt in prayer. "Old women, kerchiefs on their heads, said the rosary as tears of joy lined their faces. There were plenty of men in the church, too. Unlike some other groups, the Polish men didn't leave God for the women only." They said a Mass of thanksgiving, and then they had a block party.

The new pope settled in. He didn't, as he merrily told people, know exactly how to be pope. So he did things like hold a news conference where he walked through the crowd of journalists taking extra questions and making quips. He would get into a car and tell the driver, "Take me to the hospital," and there he would visit an old friend who'd had a stroke in Rome, and while he was there, he visited the other sick people too. Leaving the Vatican one day, he bumped into the Communist mayor of Rome and gave him a big hug, to the mayor's astonishment. Then he announced plans to visit other countries.

Yes, of course, he said, he'd like to visit Poland. He would like very much to go home.

CHAPTER THREE

"We Want God"

He went to Poland and changed the boundaries of the world.

It was the first week in June 1979, not so long ago, of course, but the political context now seems almost antique. Europe was divided, symbolically cut in two by the Berlin Wall. On one side were the democracies, which had political freedom, religious freedom, broad artistic expression, wide opportunities for education, and material affluence. But the democracies were also riddled by anxiety and self-doubt, especially among their elites. On the other side of the wall were the Warsaw Pact countries, the Communist bloc — police states controlled by the Soviet Union and run by local Communist parties. These countries, of course, had extremely limited political and religious freedom, or freedom of expression. Their economies were chronically low and ailing; what affluence there was was confined to a small minority holding high positions within the power structure.

So in the lands of freedom there was

47

comfort, opportunity, and anxiety, and in the lands of no freedom there was soul-stressing daily hopelessness, chronic want, and fear.

The new pope, who had been raised to the papacy just ten months before, was from one of the not-free countries. And as soon as he was elected, he said he would like to visit his home country to see his people.

The members of the Communist government of Poland faced a quandary. If they didn't allow the new pope to return to his homeland, they would look defensive and frightened, as if they feared that he, ultimately, had more power than they did. To rebuff him would seem an admission of their weakness. On the other hand, if they let him return, the people might rise up against the government, which could in turn trigger an invasion by the Soviet Union. The Polish government wrestled with the question and ultimately decided that it would be too great an embarrassment to refuse the pope. So they invited him, gambling that John Paul — whom they knew when he was cardinal of Kraków and who, they were sure, would not want his presence to inspire bloodshed — would be prudent. They wagered that he would understand that he was fortunate to have been given permission, and that what he owed the government in turn was deportment that would not threaten the reigning reality.

They announced the pope would be welcome to come home on a "religious pilgrimage." John Paul quickly accepted the invitation. He went to Poland. And from the day he arrived the boundaries of the world began to shift.

Two months before the pope's arrival, the Polish Communist apparatus took steps to tamp down the enthusiasm of the people. They sent a secret directive to public school teachers, explaining how they should understand and explain the pope's visit. "The Pope is our enemy," it said. It continued, "Due to his uncommon skills and great sense of humor he is dangerous, because he charms everyone, especially journalists. Besides, he goes for cheap gestures in his relations with the crowd, for instance, puts on a highlander's hat, shakes all hands, kisses children. . . . It is modeled on American presidential campaigns. . . . Because of the activation of the Church in Poland our activities designed to atheize the youth not only cannot diminish but must intensely develop. . . . In this respect all means are allowed and we cannot afford any sentiments."

The government also issued instructions to Polish media to censor and limit the pope's comments and appearances.

On June 2, 1979, the pope arrived in Poland. What followed will never be forgotten by those who witnessed it.

He knelt and kissed the ground, the dull gray tarmac of the airport outside Warsaw. At the same moment, the silent churches of Poland began to ring their bells. The pope traveled by motorcade from the airport to the Old City of Warsaw.

The government had feared thousands or even tens of thousands would line the streets.

They were wrong.

By the end of the day, counting the people lining the streets and highways plus those massed outside Warsaw and then inside it — all of them cheering and throwing flowers and applauding and holding signs and singing — more than a million people had come.

In Victory Square in the Old City the pope said a Mass. Communist officials watched from the windows of nearby hotels. The pope gave what George Weigel called the greatest sermon of his life.

Why, he asked, had God lifted a Pole to the papacy? Perhaps it was because of how Poland had suffered for centuries, and through the twentieth century it had become "the land of a particularly responsible witness" to God. The people of Poland, he suggested, had been chosen for a great role, to humbly but surely understand that they were the repository of a special "witness of His cross and His resurrection." He asked then if the people of Poland accepted the obligations of such a role in history. He asked if they were capable of accepting it.

The crowd responded with thunder.

"We want God!" they chanted. "We want God!"

What a moment in modern history: *We want God.* From the mouths of modern men and women living in a modern atheist dictatorship.

The pope was speaking on the Vigil of Pentecost, that moment in the New Testament in which there was an outpouring of the Holy Spirit on Christ's apostles, who had been waiting in fear after his crucifixion. It filled them with joy and courage. John Paul expanded on this. What was the greatest of the works of God? Man. Who redeemed man? Christ. Therefore, he declared, "Christ cannot be kept out of the history of man in any part of the globe, at any longitude or latitude. . . . The exclusion of Christ from the history of man is an act against man! Without Christ it is impossible to understand the history of Poland. . . ." Those who oppose Christ, he said, still inescapably live within the Christian context of history.

Christ, the pope declared, was not only the past of Poland, he was also "the future . . . our Polish future."

The massed crowd thundered its response. "We want God!" it roared.

That is what the Communist apparatchiks watching the Mass from the hotels that rimmed Victory Square heard. Perhaps at this point they understood that they had made a strategic mistake. Perhaps as John Paul spoke they heard the sound careen off the hard buildings that ringed the square; perhaps the echo sounded like a wall falling.

The pope had not directly challenged the government. He had not called for an uprising. He had not told the people of Catholic Poland to push back against their masters. He simply made the obvious clear. George Weigel again: "Poland was not a communist country; Poland was a Catholic nation saddled with a communist state."

On the next day, June 3, 1979, John Paul stood outside the cathedral in Gniezno, a small city with a population of roughly fifty thousand. Again there was an outdoor Mass, and again in his homily he said an amazing thing.

He did not speak of what governments want, nor directly of what a growing freedom movement wanted, nor of what the struggling Polish workers' union, Solidarity, wanted. He spoke of what God wants.

"Does not Christ want, does not the Holy Spirit demand, that the Pope, himself a Pole, the Pope, himself a Slav, here and now should bring out into the open the spiritual unity of Christian Europe . . . ?" Yes, he said, Christ wants that. "The Holy Spirit demands that it be said aloud, here, now. . . . Your countryman comes to you, the Pope, so as to speak before the whole Church, Europe and the world. . . . He comes to cry out with a mighty cry."

What he was saying was remarkable. He was telling Poland: See the reality around you differently. See your situation in a new way. Do not see the division of Europe; see the wholeness that exists and that not even communism can take away. Rhetorically his approach was not to declare or assert but merely, again, to innocently point out the obvious: *We are Christians, we are here, we are united — no matter what the communists and their mapmakers say.*

It was startling. It was as if he were talking about a way of seeing the secret order of the world.

That day at the cathedral the Communist authorities could not stop the applause. They could not stop everyone who applauded and cheered, for there weren't enough jail cells.

"What these words did was to set a historical process into motion," said Father Maciej Zieba, a writer and longtime observer of the pope. Father Zieba was an activist for Solidarity, and is now provincial of the Dominican priests of Poland. In his book *The Surprising Pope*, Zieba said, of the speech in the cathedral, "Not only did one not speak openly of European unity at that time, one didn't even think of it. It was totally beyond the horizon of the politics then practiced. It marked an epochal change in the Vatican's Eastern Europe strategy. . . ." Father Zieba quoted

Newsweek's Ken Woodward, who said a few years after the speech at the cathedral that "the jewel" in John Paul's international plans was to end the division of Europe into East and West, "accompanied by a utopian vision of a Europe stretching from the Atlantic to the Urals." Woodward said, "Only a pope from Poland could come up with such a dream."

Zieba added that it seemed at the time more than a dream: It seemed "a messianic hallucination, a naïve figment of the imagination. And besides, who out there could be bothered about Estonians, Lithuanians, or Latvians?"

John Paul could. And his dream of an undivided Europe came true.

In the summer of 2002, I spoke to Lech Walesa, the former leader of the Solidarity movement, about the impact John Paul had had on the effort for freedom. Back in the 1970s, Walesa was a stout young workingman, an ardent Catholic who worked in the Polish shipyards on the Baltic. He was not so much an anti-Communist warrior as an antirepression warrior who opposed Communist put-downs of union rights and free expression. He became an agitator for those rights. One day in the summer of

1980, during a strike action, Walesa, an electrician at the Lenin Shipyards in Gdansk, was fired for his union activities. After he was barred from the shipyard, he climbed over its walls to get inside and join with his former coworkers in an occupation strike against the Communist government. The strike was not only about union issues — low salaries and poor treatment — now it was also about freedom, about human liberty; now it was becoming a workers' revolution against the Soviet state. The workers' union, Solidarity, was born.

The Polish government eventually backed down under pressure, then allowed Solidarity to exist, then shifted its position and cracked down on the movement, making arrests. But Solidarity only grew. Walesa was arrested for a year, then released.

When I met with him in the summer of 2002, I asked him about those days, about how the Soviet Union was beaten back. Walesa was then in his sixties, thickset, his thick hair gray, his big mustache also gray. He told me, "We knew it could not be reformed — communism could not be reformed. But we knew the minute [John Paul] touched the foundations of communism, it would collapse."

The election of John Paul changed everything for Walesa and Solidarity. "A most remarkable thing: A Pole is elected pope. And he comes to Poland. And the twenty who followed me were suddenly ten million."

Walesa saw it as miraculous. "It was a greater multiplication than the loaves and the fishes."

Who removed communism from Poland? I asked. "I could . . . attribute the victory to myself," he said. "But the wonderful victory, the greatest merit, goes to heaven and the Holy Father. Thirty percent goes to Solidarity and Lech Walesa." Gorbachev "made a great contribution" by "failing to do what he intended to do." Gorbachev intended "to remodel communism." Instead, said Walesa, he let it die.

But it was the Blonie Field, in Kraków — the Blonia Krakowskie, the common fields just beyond the city — that provided the great transcendent moment of the pope's trip. It was the moment when, for those looking back, the new world opened. It was the moment, some said later, that Soviet communism's long fall began.

It was a week into the trip, June 10,

1979. It was a sunny day. The pope was to hold a public Mass. The Communist government had not allowed it to be publicized, but it was the end of the trip and Poles had spread the word. The government braced itself, because now they knew a lot of people might come, as they had to John Paul's first Mass. But that was a week before. Since then, maybe people had seen enough of him. Maybe they were tiring of his message. Maybe it wouldn't be so bad.

But something happened in the Blonie Field.

At least two million people came, maybe more, maybe three million. For a Mass in a muddy field. It was the biggest gathering of human beings in the entire history of Poland.

And it was there, at the end of his trip, in the Blonie Field, that John Paul took on communism directly, by focusing on its attempt to kill the religious heritage of a country that had for a thousand years believed in Christ.

This is what he said:

"Is it possible to dismiss Christ and everything which he brought into the annals of the human being? Of course it is possible. The human being is free. The human being can say to God, 'No.' The human being can say to Christ, 'No.' But the critical question is: Should he? And in the name of what 'should' he? With what argument, what reasoning, what value held by the will or the heart does one bring oneself, one's loved ones, one's countrymen and nation to reject, to say No to Him with whom we have all lived for one thousand years? He who formed the basis of our identity and has Himself remained its basis ever since. . . .

"As a bishop does in the sacrament of Confirmation so do I today extend my hands in that apostolic gesture over all who are gathered here today, my compatriots. And so I speak for Christ himself: 'Receive the Holy Spirit!'

"I speak, too, for Saint Paul: 'Do not quench the Spirit!'

"I speak again for Saint Paul: 'Do not grieve the Spirit of God!'

"You must be strong, my brothers and sisters! You must be strong with the strength that faith gives! You must be strong with the strength of faith! You must be faithful! You need this strength today more than any other period of our history. . . ."

And more. "You must be strong with love, which is stronger than death. . . .

When we are strong with the Spirit of God, we are also strong with the faith of man. . . . There is therefore no need to fear. . . . So . . . I beg you: Never lose your trust, do not be defeated, do not be discouraged. . . . have trust . . . always seek spiritual power from Him from whom countless generations of our fathers and mothers have found it. Never detach yourselves from Him. Never lose your spiritual freedom."

They went home from that field a changed country.

What John Paul did in the Blonie Field was both a departure from his original comments in Poland and an extension of them.

In his first comments he said that God sees one unity of Europe; he does not see East and West divided by a gash in the soil. In this way, John Paul "divided the dividers" from God's view of history.

But in the Blonie Field he extended his message. He called down the Holy Spirit — as the vicar of Christ and successor to Peter, he called down God — to fill the people of Poland, to "confirm" their place in history and their ancient choice of Christ, to confirm, as it were, that their history was real and right and unchangeable — even unchangeable by Communists.

It was a redeclaration of the Polish spirit. And those who were there went home a different people, a people who saw themselves differently, not as victims of history but as strugglers for Christ.

I believe the pope changed reality just by being the pope. In the same way the Mass at the Blonie Field changed reality just by being the Mass. Because all of those who were there would watch, later that day and that evening, the official state television reports of the event. Those reports did not show the crowds. They only showed shots of the pope standing, and sometimes speaking. State television did not acknowledge or admit what a phenomenon John Paul's visit was, or what it had unleashed.

The people who had been at the Mass at the field could compare the reality they had witnessed with their own eyes with the propaganda the state-run media reported. They could see the discrepancy. This left the people of Poland able to say at once and together, definitively, with no room for argument: *It's all lies.* Everything this government says is a lie. Everything it *is* is a lie.

And whatever legitimacy the government could pretend to, it began to lose.

One by one the people of Poland said to

themselves, or for themselves within themselves: *It is over.*

And when ten million Poles said that to themselves, it was over in Poland. And when it was over in Poland, it was over in Eastern Europe. And when it was over in Eastern Europe, it was over in the Soviet Union. And when it was over in the Soviet Union, well, it was over. And the *New York Times* could headline, ultimately, twelve years later, on August 25, 1991, GORBACHEV QUITS AS PARTY HEAD; ENDS COMMUNISM'S 74-YEAR REIGN.

All of this was summed up by the Polish publisher and intellectual Jerzy Turowicz, who had known Karol Wojtyla since they were both young men and who had gone on to be a supporter of Solidarity and member of Poland's first post-Communist government. Turowicz, remembering the Blonie Field and the pope's visit, told Ray Flynn, at that time U.S. ambassador to the Vatican, "Historians say World War II ended in 1945. Maybe in the rest of the world, but not in Poland. They say communism fell in 1989. Not in Poland. World War II and communism both ended in Poland at the same time: in 1979, when John Paul II came home."

CHAPTER FOUR

Popes Pray

Popes pray. So do you, most likely. You talk to God, thank him for what you have, ask him for blessings and graces, tell him what you're thinking about, say, "Please help me." When you say this, you feel weak and strong, alone and accompanied by armies. No one knows the power of prayer but God, of course, but John Paul's life reflected a certitude of that power.

He was praying all the time. And his prayer is said to have consisted largely of simply being with God, speaking to him interiorly, and saying, "Yes." Which, as Dostoyevsky said, is what every good prayer is.

The pope's prayer life changed over the years. Those who knew him in his later years, when pressed to guess, say they believe he prayed seven, eight hours a day. Or more.

He defined prayer as "a conversation," a "contact" with God; when he was young, his prayer consisted mostly of giving thanks and declaring his love. He told biographer Tad Szulc, "A prayer of supplication seemed to be something unworthy." Asking for things seemed too small. But as he grew older, he changed his mind. "Today I ask very much," he said.

He lost himself in prayer.

"We were to have lunch," the pope's longtime press aide, Dr. Joaquin Navarro-Valls, a psychiatrist and the head of the Holy See press office, told me. "As usual, as [John Paul] goes from his studio to the dining room he passes the chapel. He always keeps the doors of the chapel open. He does this so Christ is filling the whole house, though you don't have to say that. So one day we are together and we pass the chapel as always, and he went in for a moment to pray. Three minutes, four minutes, five minutes, twelve minutes. And eventually he looks toward me and says, 'Oh, I forgot you were here.' "

Navarro-Valls laughed. He said the fact that the pope so lost himself in prayer said a great deal about the depth of his prayer life. He offered another story. One night he was to meet the pope in the papal apartment for dinner at seven-thirty. Navarro-Valls arrived early. He walked toward the chapel and went inside, where he saw the pope, by himself. The minutes went by.

Finally, at eight o'clock the pope rose to leave. Only then did he become aware of his press aide. "It is something that he needs, to be there," Navarro-Valls told me. "When you see him there, you feel a kind of lightening, or even giddiness."

Navarro-Valls told of how he had come upon John Paul singing, by himself, in front of the tabernacle. "It is as Saint Augustine said, 'Singing is praying twice.'" Losing himself in prayer happened when the pope was out of the Vatican too. "On some occasions walking and hiking in the mountains, I would be with him and from time to time, hear a word. Always in Polish. But what I understand is a word relating to a country. His prayer has geographical dimensions! He is praying for a country that has a war or famine or want."

Every day, John Paul celebrated Mass at dawn in the chapel in his Vatican apartment. And the Mass did not begin unless he had before him his lists of the people and things he had been asked to pray for. Author and editor Father Richard John Neuhaus was sometimes with him at these times, and later, in the evening. "One thing you find out — [being with] the pope [you see] the times that are spent in prayer. Before and after meals and so forth. One of the most consistently moving to me is that usually after dinner . . . he'll go to his chapel, and he kneels before the Blessed Sacrament. Now this is his private chapel, just right off [his private rooms]. Very modest, he lives very modestly. And he kneels at [his wooden kneeler], and then you kneel behind him [in one of the small number of pews]. And he opens up the top [of his kneeler] and it's just filled, it's over-flowing, with notes people have sent him or given him at audiences. They're prayer requests, for everything under the sun. And he just kind of picks these up, rifles through them, so to speak." John Paul then prayed for the things people had asked for — a cure for a relative's illness, help in finding the right career. "You have this overwhelming sense of just how much" the requests mean to him. "He prays on specific and concrete human circumstances." He also prayed for the church. "When you consider the church, and its adversaries, and all its cultures and so forth — places that the *New York Times* doesn't deign to notice, places and people that are just a constant source of prayer and anxiety. Africa — the pope has a powerful sense of the tragedy of Africa as being forgotten in the modern world, that nobody cares about Africa." Father Neuhaus told me the pope felt the world was "callous" toward that continent. So he prayed for it. "He just kneels there and he just opens up that lid, and he leafs through. He prayerfully soldiers through, all of these worries in this church."

Others have reported a mystical dimension to the pope's prayer life. John Paul's aides had reported finding him at times lying face down on the floor of his chapel, arms outstretched like Christ on the cross. The Polish Communist government years ago noted what it called his mystical nature, and the psychological profile the CIA prepared on him in the 1970s spoke of his "mystical essence."

When asked by a journalist ten years ago how he prays, exactly what he says, the pope was both playful and serious. "You would have to ask the Holy Spirit! The pope prays as the Holy Spirit permits him to pray." Then he suggested he prays to be a better pope. And he prays, he said, about this: "The joy and the hope, the grief and the anguish of the people of our time."

I tried to imagine, after talking to these men, what the pope looked like when he is praying, what his face looked like. I mentioned this to a friend, an ardent Catholic, who replied, "But you've seen it. That look he gets when he's seated at the altar in a big outdoor Mass somewhere — when his eyes are closed and shut tight and he mutters or winces: He is praying then. He is in his interior world of prayer. Everybody's seen it. He's shown it."

What fed this prayer life?

What of the character and personality that made these prayers?

He was an intellectual and yet warm, but with an honest warmth and not just a charming one; sweet but skeptical, emotional but not sentimental. He was a philosopher whose inquiries and examinations have been called true theological breakthroughs. The American cardinal Avery Dulles, a widely respected intellectual of the church, has said that John Paul "holds a special place of eminence" as a writer and a thinker.

And yet he was a common man whose sympathies and background were with the common people. "The worker pope," they called him, because he had worked with his back in a factory as a young man.

He was a traditionalist who held high the great church thinking of the past two thousand years and insisted the teachings were true and could not be swept away by modern yearnings that the truth be otherwise. And yet he was a progressive thinker who embraced science and the arts. His thoughts on the origin of the universe were that the big bang theory of creation might well be true, that it is not incompatible with the church's teachings; that we must continue research and investigation in this area, and invite the world's scientists to understand that if the theory is true, it does not mean it was random, or an accident, or inevitable. Someone set the big bang in motion, someone made it happen, someone decreed it. (John Paul liked to remind scientists that the big bang theory was conceived in the mind of a scientist who was a priest, Father George Lemaitre of Belgium, whose work was applauded by Albert Einstein.)

He adhered to doctrine and yet encouraged dialogue; he loved the faithful and loved to tell them to reach out, with love, to those who spurn the faith. He held to the ancient teachings of the church while at the same time he was an expander and enlarger of the church's thinking. He held high the magisterium, the traditional and comprehensive teachings of the church, and yet as a writer he restated church truth in a way that seemed not crabbed or reflexive but loving, expansive, and new. He was a crusader for religious freedom and freedom of conscience.

He was a bearer of a universal message to a world he saw as broken into many different and particularized cultures, each of which, he said, took its shape from different aspects of man.

He was a transformative individual who steered the ancient church into the twenty-first century. He was a prophet: That century, he said, would be overwhelmingly religious or overwhelmingly not, but it would not be lukewarm. In this he was echoing the midcentury French philosopher and public man André Malraux.

He was the most-traveled pope in history, an apostle pope bringing the message of Christ all over the world. He was the best-selling Holy Father in history in terms of books and CDs. You could even buy CDs of him praying.

He was an old-fashioned man, a Slav born when the First World War had just ended and the Russian revolution just begun. He was born before penicillin, Lindbergh's flight, television. And yet one of his final innovations, in the summer of 2004, was the daily Vatican text message, in which he shared his thought for the day with anyone with a cellphone or a Blackberry. He enjoyed getting e-mail at john_paul_II@vatican.va.

He was a child of the twentieth century, an Eastern European. Which means he knew how to suffer. He learned early. The country he loved and was born into was enslaved by two different and yet similarly brutal gangs from 1939 to 1989, which is to say for most of his adult life. He pondered the fact of suffering in human life for many years, asked for illumination from God, and came to conclude and later write in a papal encyclical that suffering seems "essential to the nature of man." It is not random, it is not simply a matter of accident, and it is not avoidable. Suffering gives us a point in time in which "man is in a certain sense 'destined' to go beyond himself." With suffering comes always the opportunity "for rebuilding goodness in the [one] who suffers."

As a personality he was even tempered, not much given to highs and lows, had what he called a happy temperament. But there was about him, always, a sense of powerful internal control. He was often humorous, not often jolly, sometimes dry in his wit. Father Richard John Neuhaus, editor of the magazine *First Things*, told me once that when he visited the pope in Rome they joshed with each other.

How do you josh with a pope, I asked.

"He's very ethnic. He's very Polish. He finds it funny that I'm German." They made jokes about that. "There was something that had gone very well. I mentioned it, and he said, 'Pretty good for a Polish pope!' "

Once when Father Neuhaus, a New Yorker, visited the Vatican, John Paul asked him, as he always did, about the health of New York's cardinal at the time, John Cardinal O'Connor, who was not well. "So I said, 'Well, you know what Cardinal O'Connor said to me the other day? He said, "When I get up in the morning I pray that I'll go to bed that night without having discouraged any impulse of the Holy Spirit." So I said, 'Holy Father, isn't that a beautiful thing for him to say?' And the pope says, 'Yes, very beautiful. Very beautiful. But I told *him* that!' "

He loved to sing, had an encyclopedic knowledge of Polish songs, and sang one such ballad at a Mass in New York during his last visit to America. When the audience burst into applause, he gave them a

Jack Benny take: "And to think you don't even know Polish!"

He hummed when he was in a good mood. He liked to recite poetry, and he used to do it while climbing mountains.

Once during his clamorous first visit to Poland as pope, the Kraków crowds wouldn't let him go to sleep. They massed around the archbishop's residence in the dark and sang to him and called for him. The new pope came out and said, mock sternly, "Who is making all this noise?" In the laughter he told them he couldn't speak anymore because his throat was sore. Then he sang with them. Finally, at midnight, he acknowledged their demand that he speak. "You are asking for a word or two, so here they are: Good night!" Later, at a Mass in another town, he pointed out toward the Tatra Mountains and told the crowd of young people that when he had been made bishop of Kraków, he had asked his superior if he could still climb the mountains and was told yes. But now, he said, as pope, it was no longer possible. "Then stay with us!" yelled the crowd. "It's too late," said the pope. "Where were you [on the day of his election to the papacy]? Just like Poles, to try to close the barn door when the horse is gone!"

When he came to New York the first time, Ed Koch showed up to greet him. "Your Holiness, I am the mayor," he said. "I shall try to be a good citizen!" the pope puckishly responded.

At a church in Germany, at the end of a particularly effective homily that culminated in his quoting Saint Paul, the crowd interrupted him again and again with applause and cheers. "I thank you on Saint Paul's behalf!" he teased.

On his pilgrimages, when his airplane would cross the international date line, he liked to tell reporters traveling with him, with a straight face, that "now we must decide what to do with the extra day we have been given."

When his doctors would busily confer in a large group outside his hospital room after he'd been shot, he would refer to them as the Sanhedrin. "What did the Sanhedrin say today?" he'd ask his aides.

Once, as he recuperated after he had been shot, the pope told the officers of the papal household that he would like a pool to be built at Castel Gandolfo, the papal summer residence. It would be good for his health, he said; he needed now to exercise. "A pool would be expensive," said his aides. "Electing a new pope would be even more expensive," he replied. They built the pool.

He met once with a bishop who'd gained some weight. The bishop reported with pride that his diocese was quickly expanding. John Paul said, "So is the bishop!"

After his hip replacement surgery, he began to walk with a cane. Sometimes he twirled it, like a vaudevillian. Once he pretended it was a pool cue.

At a meeting of the Synod of Bishops he made his way slowly and haltingly to the front of the crowd. He looked out at the assembled prelates and muttered what Galileo had said after being forced to recant his discovery that the earth revolves around the sun. "Eppur si muove." And still, it moves.

He had the natural talents of a diplomat. He tended to defuse situations and give something to both sides in an argument while not budging from what he believed to be true. When the American bishops wrote in favor of a churchwide declaration of bias toward the poor, John Paul said yes, the poor need us, although of course we must remember that it is not helpful to divide people by class and reduce them to representatives of one socioeconomic group or another. All people are individuals, he said, and individually deserving of love. Then he moved the conversation on.

When interviewed by reporters on his airplane, Shepherd One, on the way to Central America on one of his first trips as pope, John Paul was pressed on a subject that roiled the church throughout the 1970s and 1980s. He was asked: Is it legitimate for Latin American Catholics to choose socialism? His reply was a small masterpiece of soft toughness. "We have to begin to study what socialism is and what sort of versions of it there are. For example, an atheistic socialism, which is incompatible with Christian principles, with the Christian vision of the world, with the rights of man, with morality, would not be an acceptable solution." But what about socialism that recognizes religion and guarantees its rights? "There is a lot of talk about guarantees, but you don't get to see them till later. . . . You don't see the guarantees until after the fact." He left the reporters to ponder that, and went on to other issues.

One night during his first trip to Poland, tens of thousands of young people marched to see him. They had just done something very brave. They had rescued a big cross that had once stood proudly at the top of a building of the Jagiellonian University. The government had previously torn it down. Now the students were carrying it in their hands. They asked the pope to bless it and made it clear that as soon as he did, they would march back to the university and put it in its place of honor once again. John Paul knew the government police were watching and ready to move at any sign of unrest. So he blessed the cross and then told the students not to attempt to erect it, not to provoke the authorities. They were abashed. So he joked with them until they were laughing, and the moment was defused, the potential crisis averted.

In all, one senses a paradox. So very confident, and so modest. A man born into humble circumstances who was not at all destabilized or shocked to have become the most famous man in the world. A man of pronounced views and pronounced patience. A man who used his body all his life for joy, and who accepted with equanimity his eventual inability to control that body. He believed so fully that God hears us, responds to us, intervenes in history, gives us what we need . . . and yet John Paul worked and struggled as if everything depended on him. He was extremely questioning and extremely faithful, a natural prober and thinker who naturally believed.

CHAPTER FIVE

An Immense Bell Ringing

John Paul was a Marian whose love of Christ led inevitably — according to his thinking and ardently in keeping with his nature — to love of Christ's mother. He learned his devotion firsthand, in a childhood in Poland, one of the great Marian countries.

It is interesting that the countries whose Catholics love Mary most ardently, and who have by tradition been most public in that love, have tended to be those that have known intense political oppression and poverty: Poland, Ireland, Mexico, Italy, the Philippines. Why would this be? Maybe protracted trouble helps human beings admit they need as much help as they can get, and if a father, a son, and a mother are available, they'll take all three. Maybe in part it's that families under daily duress experience more deeply the crucial importance of women because they witness it each day, in the home, and in the form of decision making and direction. When you live close to the land, you tend to absorb a strong sense of gender, of the differentness of the sexes. This might prompt the assumption that you need not only a masculine presence in your life but also a feminine one. In our world, the modern and technologized one in which we live, we like to think of men and women as the same. We even try to make them the same. But they're not the same; they are equal but different.

John Paul was captivated by Mary. He said he saw her quite literally as his mother. Since his youngest days he had worn around his neck an old brown scapular, a cloth chain with a cloth likeness of the Virgin Mary. He said it was "a help and defense in times of danger, a seal of peace and a sign of Mary's care."

He believed that she has literally intervened in human history in the many centuries since she left the world, and intensely in the past two centuries. He believed the Blessed Mother has come to us and visited us in once-obscure towns with names like Fatima in Portugal, Lourdes in France, Knock in Ireland, Guadalupe in Mexico, and that on these visits she has offered encouragement, affection, and guidance. These visitations were very real to John Paul. They were not abstract to him, or merely symbolic; they were not imagined by children and told by old ladies; they were actual moments in human history. They happened.

On May 13, 1981, when John Paul had been pope for two and a half years, he was shot in St. Peter's Square by a young man wielding a Browning 9-mm semiautomatic pistol. John Paul was in a small open-air truck that was driving slowly by the crowd that had come to see him at his weekly audience. (After the shooting, the Vatican would order the bulletproof vehicle that came to be called the Popemobile.) It was a bright spring afternoon, five o'clock. Twenty thousand people were there. He waved to and blessed them as they jumped up and down and cheered. Then he stopped the truck and picked up a little girl held toward him by her parents. He held her, smiled, handed her back, and the open-air truck moved on, heading toward the Bronze Doors of the Apostolic Palace.

Two shots suddenly pierced the air. One grazed the pope's elbow. The second struck him in the abdomen and propelled him back into the arms of his secretary, Monsignor Stanislaw Dziwisz.

The pope, conscious and in great pain,

alternately began to pray aloud and then silently on the way to the hospital. He later told the French writer André Frossard that while he was praying he realized something amazing. The moment he was shot — 5:00 p.m. on May 13th — was exactly the moment and day on which three shepherd children had first reported seeing the Virgin Mary in Fatima in 1917.

Normally in afternoon traffic in Rome, the ride to the hospital would have taken perhaps half an hour. But the ambulance carrying John Paul made it in eight minutes.

When he arrived, the pope was dying. But he was one of the few who did not think his wounds were fatal. He later said, "[A]t the very moment I fell . . . I had this vivid presentiment that I [would] be saved." In 2005, in a chapter on the shooting in his memoir *Memory and Identity*, John Paul said he had "a strange feeling of confidence" that he would live. He also said he didn't recall much of what happened when he got to the hospital. "I was almost on the other side."

His blood pressure was falling, his pulse weakening. He lost consciousness. He was rushed into an operating room at the Gemelli Clinic. As in the case of Ronald

Reagan, who had been shot in Washington, D.C., two months before, the exact nature and extent of the pope's injury was not immediately clear. The bullet that hit his abdomen had left havoc in its wake. When the surgeon made the first incision, he found blood everywhere, but the source of the hemorrhaging could not be isolated. Finally, they found there was not one wound but many: a perforated colon, five wounds in the intestines.

They operated for five hours. It wasn't clear until midnight that night that John Paul might make it, but to him the outcome was never in doubt. "One hand fired, and another guided the bullet," he later said.

He was talking about Mary.

He was certain he had been saved by the Blessed Mother. He was certain she had literally, with her hand, guided the bullet away from his main abdominal artery — which it had missed by one tenth of an inch. If that artery had been nicked or cut, the pope would have bled to death on the way to the hospital. As John Paul's biographer, George Weigel, noted, "It was a confession of miraculous intervention that the most secular soul might have been tempted to concede."

The would-be assassin, Mehmet Ali Agca, had fired at point-blank range. And yet the bullet that missed the artery also missed the pope's spinal column and every one of the clusters of nerves that lay in its path.

You know what John Paul did with the bullet that almost killed him? It had dropped to the floor of the truck and been gathered up and brought to the hospital. There, while he was recuperating, the pope asked to see it. He held it in the palm of his hand, as if weighing it. Then he directed that it be taken to Fatima, to the visitation site, and mounted in the filigreed gold crown on the statue of the Blessed Mother. You can see it there today, the brass bullet woven into all that gold. (Soon after John Paul died, as calls for his canonization increased, the Vatican announced it would reexamine the bullet to see if more could be learned about its astounding path.)

John Paul himself saw it again when he went to Fatima on May 13, 1982, a year after his shooting, in a pilgrimage he described as one of thanksgiving for his life. (He returned again in 1991 and in 2000.)

During the visitation at Fatima, the Virgin Mary had famously given three children — Jacinta Marto, her brother Francisco, and their cousin Lucia dos Santos — a series of messages. The first involved a revelation of hell, the second said that Russia would spread error throughout the world unless that country was consecrated to her Sacred Heart, and the third message is one around which some degree of controversy still continues to swirl. In 1944, Lucia, then a nun and the only surviving child of Fatima, was first asked by her superiors and then ordered by her bishop to write that message down. She did. Eventually the written message made its way to the Vatican, where it was not to be read until 1960. (Lucia said the Blessed Mother wanted it kept secret until then.)

When he was recuperating in the hospital, John Paul asked for the letter, and he read it. It said that a bishop dressed in white would be shot because of his attempts to protect the faith.

The pope — the bishop of Rome who was dressed in white the day he was shot — told friends the letter had given him much to ponder. (The third secret controversy lingers. There are those who say all of it has not been fully revealed. The Vatican insists it has. Before she died on February 13, 2005, at the age of ninety-three, Lucia, then a Carmelite nun, said it had.)

I touch again upon the supernatural. It is hard not to when writing about this pope. His life has been shaped by a series of occurrences that invite speculation — moments that seem fateful, full of portent.

No one's life is untouched by the miraculous, of course. A new father will look at his infant child's ear, as they say, and see in it a perfection and complexity that leave him speechless. To some people the life all around us every day seems full of some mysterious splendor. You walk off the street into a towering new skyscraper with high ceilings and cool air and find on the lobby floor a flower shop overflowing with perfect buds and blossoms that are vibrant and full of life. It seems like a miracle, a brilliant creation of man housing a beautiful work of God.

Beyond that, many of us, maybe most of us, have a sense that this flat world is not all there is but only part of what is. Things happen around us that we don't fully understand, for which we use expressions like "an amazing turn of events," or "I had a sort of premonition," or "It was one of those funny things."

86

Some Catholics are said to be too ready to see the miraculous or the supernatural in what may be random events, but perhaps it is truer to say that they are unusually alive to it. George Weigel, in *Letters to a Young Catholic*, has noted that in essence, Catholicism is a way of seeing the world, a distinctive way of perceiving reality. It has to do with a sacramental imagination, with seeing God in all things, and with being perhaps particularly open to the physical reality of the constant and manifold interventions of a real God in a real universe.

But John Paul's life has seemed especially touched by singular occurrences.

He was born on May 18, 1920, in the small Polish city of Wadowice. He was the third child and second boy; a sister had died either stillborn or in early infancy. His mother was Emilia and his father was Karol Wojtyla, a military clerk in the local garrison. The family lived in a modest second-floor apartment at number two Koscielna Street. The apartment was across from the parish church, Our Lady of Perpetual Help.

This is from Gian Franco Svidercoschi's *Stories of Karol*: "As she was going through labor at home, Emilia heard the hymns from the novena being held inside the church. She asked the midwife to open the windows so she could hear the singing more clearly. She then gave birth to Karol Jozef."

So the first sound he heard on earth was that of human beings singing prayers.

That was his first day on earth, which happened also to be the triumphant day that Warsaw, Poland's capital, welcomed its great liberator Marshal Jozef Pilsudski, head of state and head of the Polish army. Marshal Pilsudski had created a newly independent Poland by beating back troops of the new Soviet Union, which was attempting to take over Poland. Warsaw was full of crowds, parades, and flowers; it was a great day when Pilsudski returned home victorious from the front.

Karol Wojtyla was baptized on June 20, 1920. A few days later Lenin's army was back, advancing just outside Warsaw. The Soviets were already occupying parts of Poland. Trotsky was quoted as saying that within a year all of Europe would be Communist. The Catholic Church of Poland, sensing even then, just three years into bolshevism, what communism was, called for Polish volunteers to rise up and fight the

Russians. The volunteers came. Some arrived for duty in their World War I uniforms.

Marshal Pilsudski commanded the Polish troops and cut off the Russian advance, blunting the attack and then turning it back.

The Poles called their unlikely victory a miracle. And they thought they knew who was responsible: the Blessed Virgin, who had for a thousand years protected them. For the day of the decisive battle was August 15th, the Feast of the Assumption of Our Lady.

And to this day, proud Poles will tell you it was that victory that saved Europe from communism.

The Wojtylas didn't have much. They lived modestly. As an army clerk, Karol had a small salary, and Emilia took in work as a seamstress to make ends meet. (Here is an odd but intriguing historical fact: Ronald Reagan's mother took in work as a seamstress, and so did Margaret Thatcher's. The three great leaders most responsible for the fall of communism and the reunification of Europe spent their childhoods watching their mothers joining different pieces of fabric together and making them into a whole.)

★ ★ ★

Young Karol Wojtyla, the future pope, was always at church and usually at Mass when the great historical occurrences of his lifetime took place. When Karol was a young man considering going into the priesthood, he was in a local church, helping with Mass, when the first booms of the Nazi invasion broke the glass in the church windows all around him. That is how he found out the Second World War had begun. He was in church again when the Nazis fell. He was at Mass, and about to become a priest, when the Russian army invaded Poland as the Nazis withdrew. (He was a priest when the Russians themselves withdrew, in 1989, but by then he wasn't in Poland; he was in Rome, and he was the pope.)

The day Karol Wojtyla's immediate predecessor as pope, John Paul I, died, Cardinal Wojtyla was at Mass, in the great cathedral in Kraków. It was a High Mass and well attended because Cardinal Wojtyla was marking the twentieth anniversary of his consecration as bishop.

As seminarian, priest, and bishop, Karol Wojtyla had a special devotion to a great figure of Polish antiquity, Blessed Jadwiga.

Jadwiga was one of three daughters of a fourteenth-century king of Poland. When he died without sons, Jadwiga was to be elevated to the throne, which she did not want. The fact that she was a girl and not a boy so irritated the Polish nobility that they said they would crown her king, not queen. She was ten years old.

Soon a marriage was arranged for her by the leaders of the Polish court, who were attempting to solidify an alliance with Lithuania, which was strategically important to Poland but pagan, unlike Poland, which was Catholic. The young intended, Jagiello, grand duke of Lithuania, agreed not only to attempt an honest conversion to Christianity but to bring his country along with him. Jadwiga did not love him and did not want him; the legend has it that she fled to the great cathedral at Kraków, where she prayed on her knees for three hours before a crucifix. In the end, she agreed to the marriage after concluding its benefits to her country and her church outweighed her personal sacrifice. And so she married him at the age of twelve, in 1386. In her short life (she died in 1399) she made a great impression on her people. She was admired and loved for her sense of justice, for her warmth and patience, and for her spirit of sacrifice. She was ardent in her Christianity, a mystic. Under her and her king, Poland and Lithuania combined and became the greatest power in Eastern Europe, a robust Christian commonwealth. And together Jadwiga and Jagiello gave Kraków a great university, which helped make the city a leading intellectual center, a bridge between East and West.

So Jadwiga was a great lady, and from the earliest days of his maturity Karol Wojtyla venerated her.

In fact, he felt such a connection with her that every year on her feast day, October 16th, the anniversary of her coronation as queen, he celebrated a Mass in her honor. He did this throughout his years as bishop. And it was on her feast day in 1978 that he was elected pope. As Tad Szulc wrote, "Her name was on his lips the moment he became John Paul II."

John Paul made Blessed Jadwiga Saint Jadwiga in 1997, in an open-air Mass in Poland.

More than a century before John Paul II became pope, a great Polish poet and playwright named Juliusz Slowacki prophesied that there would be a great moment in the future when a Pole would rise to the papacy. Young Karol Wojtyla knew Slowacki's work well, had studied him in school, and had even acted in one of his plays when he was a high school and college student.

Here is what Slowacki wrote in a famous nineteenth-century poem:

Amidst all the discord,
God sets an immense bell ringing,
He opens the throne to a
    Slavic Pope . . .
Much energy is needed to rebuild the
    Lord's world
And that is why a Slavik Pope is coming
A brother of the peoples . . .

There were personal prophecies that Karol Wojtyla would someday be the pontiff.

The day he became the cardinal of Kraków, a little girl in a crowd of well-wishers blurted out that he would now be pope, and though everyone laughed, he did not, and kissed her.

There was the famous scene with the Italian mystic Padre Pio. It is a story that gained wide credence when John Paul first became pope.

Padre Pio, of San Giovanni Rotondo, a town near Naples, was a twentieth-century stigmatic who bore the wounds of Christ on his hands, feet, and side. Padre Pio was famous for his healing gifts and his ability to read souls. If you went into his confessional and didn't tell the truth about yourself, he'd remind you of the facts, quite specifically, and if you denied them, he'd throw you out. Padre Pio was said to have the gift of appearing at two places simultaneously, literally being seen by witnesses who had interactions with him in different places at the same moment. Such reports became so commonplace that sometimes when his assistant was asked his whereabouts, he'd breezily reply, "He's on bilocation."

Padre Pio was already famous by the time a young Polish priest came to see him in 1947. According to the story, when Karol Wojtyla went into the padre's confessional and knelt, Padre Pio rose from his chair and knelt at his feet, saying he would one day be a great pope.

No one seems sure if the story is true, at least no one who talks about it. There were only two people there, and both are dead. The pope did not speak of it. But he did reveal that a miracle came of their meeting. He had a close friend, Dr. Wanda Poltawska, with whom, as a young bishop, he had worked on a book about sexual ethics in marriage. But he had known her for years, since shortly after she was arrested by the Nazis and freed, five years later, from a concentration camp. In 1962, she was stricken with what doctors told her was likely a terminal cancer. She was scheduled for surgery. She told Cardinal Wojtyla, who wrote Padre Pio and asked him to pray. When X-rays were taken just before her surgery, her cancer had disappeared. Said papal biographer George Weigel, "It was, Wojtyla believed, a miracle wrought by Padre Pio's intercession, another example of the extraordinary that lay just on the other side of the ordinary."

Five years later, in 1967, Dr. Poltawska went to San Giovanni Rotondo to attend Padre Pio's early-morning Mass. She hoped to meet him, but there were big crowds. At the end of the Mass Padre Pio walked by her and stopped. "Now you are all right?" he asked. She realized he knew who she was, though they had never set eyes on each other.

John Paul named Padre Pio a saint in 2002.

There was also the incident involving the pope's friend Stefan Swiezawski, a Polish scholar and philosopher. He was visiting an abbey southeast of Rome with his wife and then-Cardinal Wojtyla during Eastertime in 1974. The abbey was called Fossanuova, and it was more than eight hundred years old. The great saint and doctor of the church Saint Thomas Aquinas had died there in 1274. In fact, the Swiezawskis and Wojtyla were there to attend a conference marking the seven hundredth anniversary of Saint Thomas Aquinas's death. Cardinal Wojtyla was saying Mass and giving as his homily an address on the two Thomases, Aquinas and the famous doubting Thomas, the apostle.

During the homily, as Cardinal Wojtyla spoke, something came over Stefan Swiezawski. It came to him "unbidden and unwilled, as if it were a kind of revelation," as he told George Weigel. After the Mass he went to his friend Cardinal Wojtyla. "You will become pope," he told him.

You would think a young cardinal being told such a thing would smile or shake his head or raise an eyebrow. Instead, he looked gravely into Swiezawski's eyes, said nothing, and walked away praying.

All these stories are about destiny, a sense that people had about John Paul that he would become a great man, a great leader. But none of those I've spoken of was the most famous of the prophets of a Polish pope. That would be Blessed Faustina Kowalska of Poland, another twentieth-century mystic, known for her communications with Christ and her exhortations regarding his mercy. She was given, she said, revelations, which she wrote down in a series of notebooks. In the sixth and final notebook, which she wrote in 1928, she said, "As I was praying for Poland, I heard the words: 'I bear a special love for Poland, and if she will be obedient to My will, I will exalt her in might and holiness. From her will come forth the spark that will prepare the world for My final coming."

Faustina too was recognized as a saint by John Paul.

These stories are captivating in a woo-woo kind of way. They suggest the possibility of an unknown and hidden meaning to things, and an unknown and hidden player in events. They suggest the existence of other realities operating under unknown conditions and by other timetables. All of which, in speaking of them, can give the impression of the imaginary, and the superstitious. Which is perhaps why John Paul didn't speak of them. He has said, simply, "[I]n the designs of Providence there are no mere coincidences."

I end with what happened after the shooting of the pope. John Paul met with Mehmet Ali Agca in his prison cell and spent two hours with him. He listened to him, told him about the Catholic faith, embraced him, and forgave him.

It was a transcendent moment of the twentieth century. The pope had been shot by a man who meant to kill him in cold blood. The man was unrepentant, changed stories about who had sent him or whether, in fact, anyone had sent him. He consistently told lies, but not consistent ones.

To this day, a quarter century later, nobody knows why Mehmet Ali Agca shot the pope, except Agca himself. The writer and investigative reporter Claire Sterling, a scholar of international terrorism, told *People* magazine at the time that Agca may have been acting on and spurred by Muslim resentment of the West, and of Christianity. "I could envision a small splinter group of Moslem fanatics with Agca among them . . . but more likely, he made the final decision alone." Later Sterling would take another view. The obvious beneficiary of a dead Polish pope was the Soviet Union, whose dominance he threatened by his very existence. Sterling wrote later in a celebrated piece of reportage that the Bulgarian secret police, in silent concern with or directly under direction from the KGB, was likely behind the assassination attempt.

Agca has told different stories. He said the Bulgarians helped him, but the Bulgarians he named were not convicted after they were brought to trial, and there was reason to believe they were never involved. (In 2002, the pope, too, said he did not see a Bulgarian connection in his shooting.) Then Agca changed his story, and changed it again. Sometimes he said he was acting alone. He said he was a professional terrorist for a Turkish fascist group of which he was a member, the Gray Wolves. And sometimes he said he'd never tell the truth.

Do you know what John Paul thought? He thought it didn't matter. Those around him have long said he showed a remarkable lack of interest in the subject. John Paul's biographer Jonathan Kwitny, in *Man of the Century*, quotes the pope's close friend Cardinal Deskur, who spoke to John Paul during the trial of the Bulgarians. Deskur said the pope told him, "I know well that the responsible one was the devil. And whether he used the Bulgarian people or the Turkish people, it was diabolical."

In 2005, John Paul spoke of his assassin in *Memory and Identity*. He said that he had forgiven his assassin even before he knew who he was, even before he arrived at the hospital to be operated on. His forgiveness was among his last thoughts before he lost consciousness.

In his memoir, John Paul called Agca a "professional assassin." That, he said, "means that the assassination was not his initiative, that someone else thought of it, someone else gave the order." Who? What group or individual? The assassination attempt, he said, was "one of the last convulsions of the 20th century ideologies of force. Force stimulated fascism and Hitlerism, force stimulated communism."

Hitlerism was no longer an "ideology of force" by the time the pope was shot, it was over. Soviet communism, which had much to gain from his death, still existed. It was, though it did not know it, in its death throes. It was capable of a "last convulsion." As for the pope's mention of fascism, that is a term whose use is often open to interpretation.

There is something Agca did before he shot the pope that in retrospect seems to suggest more meaning than the world was necessarily sensitive to a quarter century ago. On February 1, 1979, a year and a half before his attack on John Paul, Agca shot someone else. He had been part of a gang that assassinated a man named Abdi Ipekci, the editor of the most respected and influential daily newspaper in Istanbul, *Milliyet.*

Agca was arrested, and he confessed his part. And then, amazingly, he walked out of his maximum security prison, the Kartal Maltepe, in Istanbul. He just walked out, in a personal prison break that must have received assistance, the prison being a military facility and Agca having escaped in an army uniform.

Agca at this time was twenty-three years old. His family was poor, he was not well educated, and he had no money. But at this point, he began a tour of expensive travel in first-class hotels in Europe and the Mideast.

Out of jail and on the lam, he sent a letter to *Milliyet.* His subject was a planned

101

upcoming visit by John Paul to Turkey. This is what Agca wrote: "Western imperialists, fearful that Turkey and her sister Islamic nations may become a political, military and economic power in the Middle East, are sending to Turkey at this delicate moment the Commander of the Crusades, John Paul, disguised as a religious leader. If this visit is not called off, I will definitely kill the Commander-pope."

It was an amazing letter in many respects. We do not know if it truly reflected his views; it could have been written by him under the direction of communist controllers who'd gotten him out of jail and were putting in place the paper trail of a false Agca motive. Agca, when questioned about it later, said he sent the letter to distract the police from the search for him by prompting them to devote greater resources to protecting the pope during his visit. But Agca often lied. And if he was trying to divert the attention of the police from himself, it's odd that he signed his name to the letter.

After he was shot, after he had forgiven Agca, John Paul found himself pondering whether Agca understood that the man he had tried to kill had freely and fully forgiven him. He realized he wanted to tell him this himself. So during Christmas week 1983, on December 27th, the pope went to the Rebibbia prison in Rome. There he celebrated Mass. Then he went to Agca's cell, where they sat together on plastic chairs, just the two of them, and talked. Agca, amazingly, shared with the pope his confusion about how things had played out. He was a good shot, he aimed true, he had his escape planned, and yet in the end all was thwarted; how could it have happened?

Agca told John Paul that he had heard that he had shot the pope on the anniversary of the Virgin Mary's coming down to talk to children in Fatima. Yes, said the pope, it was true what he'd heard; he attributed his survival to the intercession of the Virgin. John Paul said he believed her hand had diverted the bullet Agca had shot.

Agca told the pope he was afraid of something. He feared that the Virgin would take revenge on him. He was afraid, he said, that the "goddess of Fatima" was going to kill him in his cell.

The pope listened. He told Agca the story of Fatima, explaining that Mary wasn't a goddess and wasn't vengeful; he said she was the mother of God and that she loved Agca. He should not fear her, John Paul told him.

Later the pope would say that he felt he had reached Agca. "Ali Agca — as I believe — understood that above his power, the power of shooting and killing, there is a greater power. He began looking for it. I wish for him that he finds it."

And so the pope talked to and allayed the fears of the man who had tried to kill him. That moment — the two of them sitting on plastic chairs in a prison cell — is a great moment. If goodness could be concentrated into light, one of the most brilliant and radiant flashes of the past century happened in that little cell in the Rebibbia prison.

The story ends with what happened to the pope in 2005, as he was dying. In February he was hospitalized for ten days because of difficulty breathing, which was said to be connected to the flu. While in the hospital he received many letters and notes. One, which wished him good health and a quick recovery, was from Mehmet Ali Agca. And on April 2nd, when he died, one of the first requests to attend the funeral came from Agca. Prison officials turned him down.

CHAPTER SIX

Closer

I want here to mention the personal. One of the reasons I came to love this pope is that I began my journey to serious Catholicism, to deepened belief, during the time that he was the leader of the Catholic Church. And so I watched him more closely than I had any previous pope; I listened to him, learned from him. I took his observations as advice, and his actions as inspiration.

In time, I came to realize that I was experiencing him as a spiritual father. It took me years to understand that that was how I saw him.

We all want a spiritual father. We want someone who can inspire and guide us in the most important area of life, our very understanding of its meaning. So many of us did not have fathers who could teach us about faith and the deeper meaning of things, or who could teach us effectively or through demonstrating faith. For my parents, just existing, just keeping their heads above water, absorbed all their energies. My father himself had not been taught what to believe, why to believe it, what is true, what should be honored.

I came to see that John Paul was coming to play that role in my life, as I am certain he did for millions, tens of millions, of others.

A spiritual father is more than someone you admire. He is someone with whom you feel safe, because he can point the way to truth, which somehow we all know is the only safe thing in the world.

And so let me tell you my John Paul stories.

I would see him on television and in magazines — gazing out at crowds, bowing his head in prayer, saying Mass, gesturing from a balcony in his weekly audience, waving at people as he passed through some city street in the Popemobile. And whenever I would see him, I would stop whatever I was doing, without thinking, and watch. Always I would be moved in some way I did not understand. Once, at the sight of him on TV, I began to weep, and then I sobbed, and I did not know why. And at these moments, when I was moved, I would always think of another picture, not of him but of someone else.

It was early in his papacy, on John Paul's

first trip back to Poland. That country then was a rougher-looking place than it was before and is now. It was still in its own way premodern. When the pope spoke at the Mass in the Blonie field, the land was trampled, large parts of it turned to mud. There was a picture of a woman that I saw in *Life* or *Look* magazine. She was there in the Blonie Field. She was old — seventy or so, but old-fashioned old, with wiry gray hair. She was dressed in long, dark, nondescript clothes, with some kind of peasant scarf on her head. She looked like a European who had nothing. She was standing alone in the mud, but she was gazing up at the pope, who was in the far distance; and she had a look on her face that said she was really seeing something.

And I saw that picture — I did not keep it, and have been thinking of it and looking for it for twenty-five years, in old magazines — and I thought: I know who she is. She is someone I know. I thought without saying it to myself: She is me.

Then, at that time in my life, as a young woman, I was in the mud and looking into some far distance. Somehow my heart and my head knew that what was big and beyond me was true, but I didn't act on the truth, or include it in my life, or allow it to direct me.

So many times in so many ways over the past twenty-five years I would go back and forth. I would follow the implications of my interior knowledge and embrace belief, and read great classics of religious thought, reach out to those who, it seemed to me, were more knowledgeable, more highly evolved. I would go to church and pay attention. I liked being there. And then I would step back, and stop, and become immersed again in the stupid and alluring world of No Belief. The French in another context call this "nostalgia for the mud." They mean a bourgeois romanticization of impoverishment, which is to say they mean it to some degree in economic terms. But I mean it in spiritual terms. Every time I recognized the truth and lived it, I was happy, and when I did not, I was not. And yet I always returned to not-happy, as if that were . . . warm and happy mud.

Once, as those days continued, but in a way reached their end, I talked with a man — he was a conservative intellectual, impressively bright, censorious by nature — who asked me over drinks if I believed in God. "Yes," I said, sturdily. He said, "And in Christ?" I said yes. He said, "Really? Do you think if you died now, you'd go to heaven?" I was surprised by this question but said yes, and he laughed. He said, "Why?" And I don't recall what I said, but I remember what I thought. I thought: *Because I love God and mean well and He knows.*

This struck me as news, that I loved God, for I don't think I'd ever thought that before. Or that I believed I meant well.

I was, as I say, not schooled in the church. Like many American Catholics of my generation, the boomers, I sort of slipped off the plate in terms of the inculcating of belief. So many of our parents were first- and second-generation immigrants from Europe who grew up in Brooklyn, Baltimore, Boston. They had been taught in a rigorous old-world school in which ethnicity seemed to have as much to do with who they were as faith. Many of them came to see the old Catholic ways as immigrant ways. What they wanted was America. Theirs was the age of FDR, Freud, *All Quiet on the Western Front*, the Great Depression. They went off to World War II, experienced the Europe their parents had left, and came back too cool for the room.

My father had only one childhood religious memory that he shared. The day he showed up for his first communion, as a child of eight or so — a little Brooklyn street urchin with no father and a mother who neglected him — a priest or a brother, who were more numerous then, saw that my father had broken a rule. All the children had been told to wear white suits and white shoes. My father had worn brown shoes, the only ones he had. The priest or brother saw my father on line, saw his shoes, and hit him on the head with his fist. An ex-Catholic was born.

My mother, too, associated Catholicism with unhappy things, though she was not clear as to why. They married in 1947, my father just home from the war, and one belief they seemed to hold in common was that organized religion was for the old-fashioned, for hypocrites and creeps who would hit you on the head for wearing the wrong shoes.

They wanted to be modern. They wanted to leave their not-adequately lit apartments behind and enter the American sunlight. And while the church held little for them, other areas of life, which might even be called competing areas, seemed more alluring. My parents were born at roughly the same time as the American movie industry, in the mid-1920s, and during their most impressionable years, in the late thirties and forties, when the world was most vividly imprinting itself on their young brains, the images they absorbed were not those of statues or religious art but celluloid images, cinematic pictures. And they developed, I think, an imaginative reverence for the images they saw. Their icons were not the Blessed Virgin or the Infant of Padua but Joan Blondel and Bogie and Gable and Cagney and Bette Davis. We did not as a family go to church, but we never missed the Academy Awards.

All this made a big impression on me, but there is another countermemory that made a bigger one. I had an old aunt, my maternal grandfather's sister, a girl from Donegal, in Ireland, who went to church every Sunday and who had religious cards and rosary beads in her room. Her name was Jane Jane. She visited us sometimes. I liked when she was there. She brought order. She made dinner and cleaned the house and was happy to see us when we came home from school. Sometimes as she walked along the street what she was thinking would escape her, and I would hear her praying aloud. She was eccentric, poetic, believed. I don't remember her teaching me about Jesus or the saints or God or heaven. I just remember her being, and my absorbing her being, her way of being alive. She saved my life. In a chaotic household roiling with unhappiness and illness, she would visit and bring calm.

I could tell she had something, and I could tell it was good. So I started to think, when she took me to church, "Maybe nice people go here," or "Maybe if you go here, you become nice."

In 1992, I met a man who inspired me, and I met him, as often happens in such stories, at a time that others were inspiring me.

I had joined a Christian Bible study group with some intelligent women, mostly Protestant, who were to one degree or another desperate to believe in something, but it had to be the truth. (They'd already tried the nontrue, and it hadn't worked.) We had weekly meetings. They were important to me, in part because I learned so much about what was in the Bible — I hadn't really known — and also because as people got to know one another, they shared their lives and experiences, and I learned from those too.

You would think — I suppose everyone

thinks, and I thought, as well — that Christians in Bible study would be mild ladies recounting their tidy sins. Boy, was that not true. These were women who'd been through modern life — they had lived the seventies and eighties, they hadn't kept themselves apart and protected from the culture but had jumped right in, and their conversation was as interesting as a modern novel. More so, actually, more interesting and richer and deeper because they had experienced or were experiencing conversion, which had changed their lives, and now they had a context in which to frame their experiences. Their stories were wonderful — drunken car accidents, domestic violence, abortions, infidelities, the reappearance after twenty years of an illegitimate child. It was better than television.

Here's something that may surprise you: When one of those stories comes along where the New Jersey high school girl has a baby in the bathroom during the prom and then throws it in the trash so she can go back and keep dancing — when those stories come along, some people have a good time condemning the high school girl. But my Bible study ladies never condemned the high school girl. They were the last to be surprised by sin, or to feign surprise.

There was also this that I noticed. My friends who were sophisticated nonbelievers, who were professionals and journalists, were always talking about others. "Her children don't speak to her." "He's gay." "She married him for money." But the Bible study women were talking about themselves. They weren't judging others.

They all knew — they had come to the conclusion along the way — that the lives they had previously lived were unwhole, not in accord with the peace that they somehow knew or intuited was out there, and available, and summoning.

Some of them occasionally seemed swept up by the embarrassment of their lives: "I find it hard to believe I did that." And some seemed to wrestle with guilt. But those who'd been Christian for a long time and lived their belief, seemed beyond that. As if embarrassment at one's life was not only beside the point, and boring, and even rather vain, but was itself unwhole, not good, not . . . of God. They thought it was of the evil one, as they say. Anyway, the general idea seemed to be, as Lucianne Goldberg once said of George Bush, "What happened before Jesus stays with

Jesus." He forgives everyone who seeks it. Who are you not to forgive yourself?

But I meant to be telling you about a man I met who inspired me. His name was Leonard Cheshire. Cheshire was a great man, though not much known in America. He had been Group Captain Leonard Cheshire, a hero of World War II, one of the most decorated airmen in the history of the Royal Air Force.

I interviewed him for *Mirabella* in 1990, when I was writing a column for that good magazine. We met in Manhattan at the Madison Hotel, for drinks. He was visiting America to promote an idea he had for turning old weapons of the cold war into small metal symbols of peace. He was tall and slim and held himself in his dark suit with an erect bearing. His thinning gray hair was combed back straight. He was seventy-three years old. And our conversation turned quickly, though I can't recall why, to religious faith.

In a soft voice and with a striking humility, he told me about his life. In early July of 1945, his brother, Christopher, also an airman, who had been shot down in 1941 on the way back from a bombing run on Berlin and held prisoner by the Nazis in Poland, was released and had returned to

London. Leonard met him there and welcomed him home. They went for drinks to the Mayfair Hotel with a group of friends who were also veterans of the war. The evening was boisterous, but in time the conversation turned serious. They — the young, sophisticated, and well-educated men who'd just been through fighting a hellish war, as their fathers had almost thirty years before — found themselves arguing about God. They asserted, one after another, that God didn't exist.

"I tried to change the conversation," Lord Cheshire told me. And then he found himself saying this: "You're talking nonsense. God is a person, and you know it!"

And suddenly *he* knew it.

He didn't know he knew that. He'd never thought about it.

A week before, still in the service, he had been briefed for the first time about the atomic bomb, which the Americans had just used on Hiroshima and Nagasaki. "So I was coming to terms with the realization that God really does exist, and what am I going to do with that information, and coming to terms with the nuclear age."

He was thinking to himself, he told me, "I'm one of the lucky ones. There were those who didn't make it. I couldn't just settle for a nicely paid job or staying on in the air force." But he wanted to make the world better.

He joined the Church of England, but "it did not have the answers I was looking for." He continued to look for a spiritual home, and then a few years after the war ended, an epochal event that didn't look big at the time — only frustrating — occurred. A friend of his was desperately ill and needed somewhere to stay. There was no place that could or would take him, and so Cheshire decided to take him to his home in Hampshire, in southern England, to care for him there. This was the beginning of Cheshire's lifelong mission to help the disabled live in dignity in what came to be known as Cheshire Homes, of which there are now hundreds throughout the world.

After a lifetime of working with the sick and disabled, he came to believe, as he later said, that their suffering was not pointless, and not at all without meaning. He came to believe that their suffering had a mission "to draw out the inherent good will that is in all of us, and so to make us forget ourselves and draw closer to one another in our common journey through life."

I would often think of those words in the early years of the twenty-first century as I watched old John Paul.

Cheshire was famous as a good man, though he did not see it that way. He saw himself simply as part of something, a small piece of a larger fact. And when I met him in 1992, he told me what he had learned in his life. "I now know that God has a plan for each of us. The thing is to find out what it is." How? "Through prayer, through keeping your mind open, and through the circumstances of daily life and the people you meet."

As I took this in, he added, "I further know that if God has something special for you, you have a knowledge of it inside you, which causes you not to be satisfied with anything that isn't this thing." You're "restless" until you find it, he said.

I want to bring John Paul back into this, for he was ever in the background of my thoughts and experiences in those days when I was coming to regard him as a spiritual father.

I see now new meaning in the first two times I ever set my eyes on him in person. The first time he was far away from me, and I could barely see him. The second time he was closer; I could have touched him. These two facts — far away, closer — seem to me to have an underlying meaning.

The first time I saw John Paul was on his first trip to America, in 1979, when he was a new pope. I was at that time a young writer and producer on the radio side of CBS News, and I was lucky to be assigned to be one of the producers for the live network coverage of the pope's appearance at St. Patrick's Cathedral in New York.

I got all dressed up in a brilliantly attractive suit, but I was not doing it for the event, or the church, or the pope. I had other things on my mind — a lovely man — and I was on my way to mischief. I promise you I did not care. I only cared that it was very glamorous to be all dressed up, on assignment, and in St. Patrick's, which was full of attractive and important people.

When I got to St. Pat's, I was wearing around my neck an aluminum chain from which dangled the media credentials that media folk like myself wore to get past the regular people waiting on line. I was respectfully waved in at a series of checkpoints. It was clear I was a very important person. I looked excellent in my dark red silk blouse and my shimmering charcoal gray suit, accessorized by my plastic ID tags with CBS NEWS written all over them.

I got to the place where I was supposed to work, with the technicians and some reporters, in the back of the cathedral. Our lines were up and working, the technicians had done their jobs, the reporters were waiting to report the entrance of the pope. There was really nothing for me to do. Except stand around looking glamorous in my black high heels.

I got bored, wanted to see more, and thought it would be nice if more people could see how good I looked. So I walked away from our work area. I walked out a big side door of the cathedral and stood on the great marble standing area, beyond which are the great marble steps on the side of the cathedral. I stood there looking out at the throng — the people with no tickets, no credentials, no IDs with a network news logo on them. I stood there looking at them with my arms folded, important insider that I was.

"Move on." It was a police officer in a sharp black hat. Middle aged, stern looking. He was talking to me.

"Hi, Officer." I was cool. He must be confused. "I have ID; I'm with CBS."

"I don't care. Move on. Outside."

I was startled. He didn't seem to know I was important. He didn't seem to care. No, more than that: I had the distinct and immediate feeling he didn't like my type.

And I got that bad feeling you get when Information That Is True suddenly comes to you. I thought, and then ejected from my mind the thought, *I am a type. And I wouldn't like my type either.*

He shooed me from the steps. I joined the crowd outside and waited in line and got to the checkpoints and past the guards and ran in late to be with my colleagues, who were not amused at my lateness.

Well, the pope came, and we reported it, and I went on with my life; but I was in a dark time, though I did not know it, and I couldn't help feel, in the days and years afterward, that I got shooed from the cathedral because I didn't deserve to be there.

In fact, I still think that's true.

And years later as I actually became serious about life and what is expected of us and what is true, I'd think: *I was being told that day what a mess I was. I didn't listen. But I did hear.*

The pope's second trip to America came in 1995. This time I really wanted to see him, wanted to rest my eyes on him; I wanted to feel the constriction in my chest when he went by.

I was no longer with CBS or any other organization, just a book writer working at home. I didn't know what to do to get to see him, to get into any of the big masses he was holding, so I simply prayed on it. A few days before the pope's visit, I mentioned to my friend Nancy Dickerson Whitehead that I was hoping to see him and was asking God for help, but so far I was coming up zero.

"What are you doing besides praying?" she said.

"Mmm, not much really." She reminded me of the story of the man in the flood who ran to the roof as the waters rose. He prayed to God for help, knowing it would come. And because he knew it would come, when a tree floated by and he could have jumped on it to float to safety, he didn't. And when a big door floated by on which he also could have floated to safety, he let it pass. Then an empty canoe actually came by, floating out of someone's garage.

The man waited for God's help. And then it got dark and he got cold and scared, and he raised his fist in frustration.

"I had faith in you, God, and you didn't help me!"

And suddenly there was a voice, and God said, "I sent you a tree, a door, a canoe!"

So she told me: Get rocking.

I thought this good advice and started calling everyone I knew who might be able to help. And the next day, of course, I got a call from Nancy Dickerson Whitehead, who'd mentioned my plight to a friend who had two tickets to see the pope at St. Patrick's Cathedral and couldn't use them.

It was fabulous. I thanked her profusely and accepted them and called my sister who lives in Staten Island and asked her to come with me. She had told me a story twenty-five years before of being on a bus stuck mysteriously in Midtown. The bus was in a huge traffic jam and didn't move for half an hour; the passengers didn't know why until they saw police lights and limousines coming down Fifth Avenue and then — the pope! It was Paul VI, on his visit to America. My sister never thought she'd see a pope. Neither did the rest of the people on the bus, many of whom were Hispanic, who began to say out loud, "El Papá!"

The way she described it, it was clear

she'd never forget it. But she couldn't come to see the pope this time and begged off; it wouldn't work.

This was sad. Who deserved it more? So then I said to God, *Please tell me who I should bring.* And the person who came to mind was a woman I knew in New York, a Democratic Party fund-raiser and activist who had told me once at a party that she was enormously moved by the pope.

So I called her and asked if she'd like to go. She was so grateful and excited that I knew I'd invited the right person. It felt good.

The day came. It was on the weekend. There had been only one snag: On the day the pope was at the cathedral, my friend had planned to be away for the weekend with her family in Martha's Vineyard. But don't worry, she said; she wanted to see John Paul so much that she would rent an airplane, fly into Newark, and meet me at 2:15 p.m., a block from the cathedral, where people with tickets were to meet.

The service was to begin after 3:00 p.m., but they would close the doors at 3:00, we'd all been warned. Be early.

I got there at 2:00. She wasn't there at 2:15 or 2:30. She wasn't there at 2:45. And she wasn't there at 2:55.

I was in a kind of agony, straining to see all the way down the avenue, hoping she'd materialize out of the mist.

The minutes ticked by, and now I had to make a decision. The woman who took the tickets at the barricade told me no, she couldn't hold the ticket for my friend; I'd have to decide now whether to go in or not. "They're closing up."

If I didn't move ahead now and walk into the cathedral, they'd close the doors and I'd never get in.

As she said this, I started to hear in the distance a great cheer. It was my pope, my darling pope who had flown in from Italy to see us, proceeding down Fifth Avenue in his Popemobile. The crowds, hundreds of thousands of people, were now cheering as he rode by.

Oh, God, what to do. I wanted so much to see him, and yet I couldn't have a good time, couldn't concentrate, without my friend, who I knew was a responsible and effort-making person and who would never let me down lightly. If she was late, there was a reason. I couldn't leave her out here.

I prayed: *Oh, God, send her, send her.*

And now it was three o'clock.

And they closed the doors.

I looked down Madison Avenue again,

and there running toward me was a woman with blond hair blowing in the wind and big black marks under her eyes. She'd been crying. She was crying because they'd circled over Newark for more than an hour; it had been terrible, there'd been fog, she knew she'd missed the pope —

No, no, I said; it's fine, let's run, you never know.

And we ran, together, holding hands. And we got near Fifty-first and Fifth, and the pope was entering the sealed cathedral. A great roar from the jam-packed crowd outside, of which we were now a part.

We saw him, sort of. In his Popemobile, as he went by . . .

Well, we settled in, standing with tens of thousands of people. As a police officer would come by, we'd say, "We have tickets; is it possible to let us in?"

"No, sorry, all shut down."

Well, we'd listen on the loudspeakers. It wasn't terrible. The pope would speak and we'd hear him.

There was a woman crying. She was standing to my right and crying out loud with a hankie in her hand. She had a teenage daughter with her. I turned to her, and we spoke. She was crying because they had tickets but had arrived late. They had

126

come all the way from Chile to see the Holy Father. They had flown on a plane from Chile!

We joined together and commiserated, shared our stories. Then two college girls joined us. They were sad too, not that they had tickets but that they'd come to New York and hoped for a glimpse and hadn't gotten one. . . . Then to my left I saw a New York social figure, a philanthropist, a lovely woman standing by herself behind a barricade, looking lost. She had a ticket too. She'd gone to the wrong door, been redirected to the wrong place, and now couldn't get in. . . . She was white haired and trembling, and I put my arm around her, and we, too, commiserated and stood waiting, listening for the pope's voice.

Now and then some official-looking person would come by and we'd ask for help, but we got nowhere.

And then suddenly:

A handsome young man in a gray suit, tall, with dark hair, walked across the street from the cathedral and stood before me at the barricade.

"Are you Peggy Noonan?" he said.

Yes, I said.

He moved the barricade forward. "Come," he said.

Whoever he was, he was in charge and he could help us. But I didn't understand, so I just looked at him.

"I read your stuff sometimes," he said. "Come." He moved his head at the cathedral as if to say, "I'll get you in."

I hesitated. To go in I would have to leave my friends — the Democrat, the sobbing Chilean and her daughter, the college girls, the philanthropist. And we all wanted so much to see our pope, and no one of us deserved it more than any other.

"Go!" said the Democrat, so happy for me.

But love came into me, which brought faith, which brought strength. I put my arms around my friends. "We are all here together," I said to the man. "We must stay together, please."

And he thought for a second. And said nothing. And then he opened the barricade wider.

And we ran, all of us.

We ran across the street holding hands, hair flying, and they let us in the side door, near the middle of the block. As we ran in, I turned to thank the man. He had come with us just to the door, and there, in the small crowd at the door, I yelled to him, "Thanks, what's your name?"

"Detective Kelly," he yelled, and smiled. And I turned to my friends and then turned back to him once more, and he had disappeared into the crowd.

We entered the bubbling cathedral. We were pushed forward into a jostling section near the altar. And just as we were pushed in, great cheers were coming from the main aisle of the cathedral, and now there was movement at the steps of the altar and we turned and saw . . .

There he was.

Our pope, radiant. With everyone cheering. He was just a few feet away from us.

And we could not believe our good fortune, and we wept and laughed and squeezed one another's hands. He said a Rosary, on his knees. We said the Rosary with him, standing.

And it was beautiful. And none of us will ever forget that day.

Afterward I thought: *The first time I saw him in this place I was living destructively, and I was thrown out. Now in my life I have been trying to live constructively. And I was thrown in.*

Let me tell you something that just occurred to me as I have been writing this: The door I was thrown out of and the door

I was thrown into: I think they were, literally, the same door.

In the years afterward I could not help but think that those two events were not accidents; they were both expressions of a reality deeper than I could see and more surprising than I could guess.

CHAPTER SEVEN

Finding Him

You may wonder at what point I actually felt that I had become so immersed in my faith that it was I and I was it — when it had all clicked together. I don't know. I think finally coming to believe in Christ is like getting well after an illness: You can't say at exactly what point the recovery commenced, but you know when you're getting better and stronger, and at the end you know when you've recovered. But here is something I began to feel after I had faith: the unexpected joy of living things. At some point, living things began to seem precious to me, and I wanted to pet them, hug them — babies and dogs and lizards, whatever. For me the great fruit of belief is joy. There is a God, there is a purpose, there is a meaning to things, there are realities we cannot guess at, there is a big peace, you are part of it. "God is good." Near him is where you want to be. There is something called everlasting happiness, and Saint Paul, a fiercely imperfect man who was a great man, was granted visions of it, and that great user of words was floored by it and said that no one can imagine how wonderful it is, the human imagination cannot encompass it. Or, as Dante wrote, "The beauty I beheld transcendith measure/Not only past our reach, but surely I belief/That only He who made it enjoyeth it complete."

In 1996 a friend wrote and asked me how I would answer the question "How do you find God?" I thought about it awhile and sent this reply.

Finding God is not hard, because he wants to be found. But keeping God can be hard. He wants to be kept, of course, but for most of us finding him and keeping him is the difference between falling in love and staying in love. The latter involves a decision that is held to.

Here is a path to finding him and keeping him.

One: Get yourself in trouble. Let life make you miserable. This shouldn't be hard. "A bad night in a bad inn," Teresa of Avila is said to have described our earthly life; and every smart, happy, well-adjusted adult you know would probably admit that that's just about right. So get low, gnash your teeth, cry aloud, rend your garments, refuse to get out of bed. Be in crisis.

Trouble is good. "Man's extremity is God's opportunity," as American evangelicals say. But before they said it, Henry VIII's first wife, Catherine of Aragon, said it. "None get to God but through trouble." For most of us, the world with all its dazzlement has to turn pretty flat and pretty dry before we want God. But God seems to turn it flat just at the moment when he knows we're ready. So embrace your ill fortune as a blessing. (If you haven't been blessed with a crisis, I'm not sure what to tell you beyond pray for one. You may have to just hang around enjoying the dazzlements until he's ready to lower the boom. But he will, in his time and not yours, if that's the only way he can get your attention. Because not only are you looking for him, but he's been looking for you.)

Two: Once you're so low you're actually on your knees, review the situation. You could start by admitting what you've long sensed and avoided knowing: that many of the joys and delights of the world are fleeting, and some are fraudulent, and that even though those who know you best would never think this, you happen to have noticed lately that you have a rather black heart. Don't let this be demoralizing: Everyone has a black heart. As a brilliant (and agnostic) publisher recently remarked to me in a conversation about why war occurs, "Because there's something wrong with us." There is. It's inspiring how much good people actually do considering who and what we are.

Three: You're miserable and convicted and still on your knees. Address the God whose existence you doubt. Ask for his help. Ask for his forgiveness. Ask for his mercy. Ask to know him. Or ask a saint to get you to him. (All saints have had dark nights.) Evangelical Protestants sometimes use words like these: "Lord, this hasn't worked with my being in charge, so I give my life to you. I believe in you. Help me to believe in you. I ask you to be in charge of my life." I think these are great words. They are not a prescription for passivity. They are an acknowledgment of reality and a pledge of obedience, which can be quite arduous. Belief ain't for sissies.

One evangelical friend uses the image of a throne. Either God is on the throne of your life or you are. You don't belong on it. He's the king. You're the servant. He's the Father. You're his child. Let him sit there. Every time you, in your pride and stupidity, try to claw your way back into control, remember the throne, and offer the seat to the gentleman who is older and wiser than you.

Four: Pray. A priest to whom I'd gone once for guidance told me that prayer is just conversation with your Father in heaven, and like any good conversation with an intimate, it should be honest, trusting, uncensored. Tell him anything — what kind of day you had, a triumph, a temptation, something that's nagging at you. Ask for his blessing for an endeavor. Give thanks. Share frustration.

Prayer in my experience is hard, easier to think about than do. In one way, I pray a lot, all day, in a continual conversation. But concentrated prayer is hard. People who know tell me to make time in the morning or evening, a half hour or so, to read the Bible and engage in sustained and concentrated prayer. I know they're right. I'll tell you something I started to do a few years ago that is connected to this and has made an enormous difference for me. I started reading the New Testament and asking God that I be allowed to know that what I was reading actually happened, that it was all true. During this time, the Acts of the Apostles came alive for me, and after that everything else did too.

Five: Get yourself some friends who will support you and help you. Go to church and find out if there's someone there — a priest or layperson — who helps converts, for if you're looking for God, you're having a conversion experience. If your local priest is busy, and chances are he is, find out what's available to believers at your church — daily prayer meetings, for instance — and go. And talk to people. Ask about retreats — two or three days away, usually in a religious setting — with people who want to enliven their spiritual life. It's hard to go on a retreat, and yet I've never heard anyone regretting it. I've never heard a person say, "I wish I hadn't gone to that retreat."

Six: See if you can find and get into a Bible study group to learn more about what you believe in, or a prayer group.

Seven: Read — for knowledge and to enliven the spirit. Books that were important to me: Thomas Merton's memoir of his conversion, *The Seven Storey Mountain; Saints for Sinners* by Alan Goodier; *To Know Christ Jesus* by Frank Sheed; *My Utmost for His Highest*, the book of daily devotionals by Oswald Chambers that evangelicals read. In fact, just about any born-again Protestant book is good. They are wonderful for their personal sense of redemption and their excitement about Christ. Don't fuss with doctrinal complexities if you're sophisticated enough to see them — I wasn't as a rule — as doctrinal disputes are not your problem right now, and anyway, God will heal them all in time. "The issue becomes the icon," the chaplain of the U.S. Senate once told me. He meant: Love Jesus and leave the commentary to others.

Eight: If you never get very excited by your conversion but just plod through, good for you — you'll get your joys. If you start out with excitement and it flattens or lessens — and it probably will — pray for ardor, ask for your old thirst, and keep plugging. It's the most important thing in your life. And remember, every time you fall or fall away, ask for help. You'll get it.

Nine: Watch John Paul. He seems to say something every day about belief. It's as if he wants to tell us something before he leaves.

After the pope came to America and I said the Rosary with him in St. Patrick's, I longed to meet him. I wanted to go to

Rome and simply touch his hand.

And finally I did. It was late June 2000.

Let me tell you what it was like to meet him. It was like what the actor Richard Burton said of Winston Churchill: "The force of his presence was like a blow to the heart."

I was to be in Rome to make a speech to a professional group about the upcoming American elections. After I was invited to participate, I called a woman I'd recently met who worked in the office of Cardinal O'Connor of New York. I asked if she knew if the pope would be in Rome in June and, if so, how did one get into a public audience. She told me yes, the pope was scheduled to be in Rome and the cardinal himself would be too, and she would ask him to help me.

Indeed he did.

I was in Rome for five days. Each day I hoped a call would come, and each day it didn't. The day before I was to leave, on a Thursday morning, the phone rang in my hotel room and a woman with an Italian accent and perfect English told me that the next morning I would see the pope. "Go to the bronze doors of the Vatican," she said, "and wait."

That's what I wrote in my notes. No address, just "big bronze doors, Vatican."

The next morning at sunrise, already awake and showered and having found somewhere a light scarf to wear on my head, I hailed a taxi and said in English with no confidence, "The big bronze doors of the Vatican, please." To my surprise, the driver said "Okay!" as if people often asked for that destination, and took me on a ten-minute ride through almost trafficless streets.

I stood in front of two big bronze doors and waited alone in the sunlight. Then I knocked. The sound of my knock was tinny, almost comic, against the heavy tonnage of the doors. No one answered.

Soon a young man came by — early twenties, tight black T-shirt, tight black jeans, earrings up and down the lobes of his ears, a ring in his brow, black spiky hair, sideburns shaved to points on the curve of his jaw. Tattoos on the top of his arms disappeared under his T-shirt. He looked like a heavy-metal rocker. We waited quietly, looking like loiterers. He looked at me and then looked away. I looked at my watch. "Guess they're not open yet."

He nodded and said, "I'm early."

"Do you have an appointment this morning?"

"Yes," he said. "I'm going to see the pope."

Now I noticed that suspended on his chest was a silver crucifix, four or five inches long, hanging from a rough leather chain.

He was from Canada, he told me. He wrote rock music. He loved John Paul. He was in Rome for work and asked his bishop in Canada if he could see the pope.

I told him I had done the same.

And little by little more people appeared. A hearty middle-aged man with an Australian accent in a black suit, his wife and teenage children. He looked like the richest Catholic in Sydney.

Then a Polish family came. The children were in full traditional costume, with blond hair and big bows — five children in old Polish dress, and their parents in modern dress.

More people arrived, and soon there were more than a dozen of us.

Suddenly, silently the great doors opened, and we were gestured in by a man in a gray janitor's uniform, and hustled up the stairs, past Swiss Guards, up marble stairs, to the right and up more marble stairs. Then a landing with great marble halls, then up another floor of marble stairs until we were ushered into a big room of white-gray marble, with big windows and big brown doors.

Inside there were more people, groups of people, waiting. There were about thirty of us in all. We stood against the walls lining the room.

There was excited chatter, soft laughter. I had stuck with my heavy-metal Canadian, and the Australians had stuck to us.

The Canadian looked at me and said, "What do we do when we meet him? How do you meet the pope?"

It hadn't occurred to me to think about this, so I shook my head and said, like an idiot American, "I think you shake his hand."

He said, "You do? I thought you, like, kiss it. Or bow."

"I don't know," I said, and turned to ask the Australian burgher —

Suddenly there was silence, as if an unheard signal had been given, and we turned our heads and looked in the same direction, toward the doors in the corner. They opened, and the pope shuffled in. He was both massive and frail, full and bent, like frail marble. He walked slowly, with a cane. The room burst into applause. A little group of dark-haired young nuns in blue, over to the left, spontaneously began to sing. They were so happy to see him they were shouting out song, and he stopped still in front of them. His head went back a little, and he took his cane and shook it toward them comically and said, in a baritone that filled the room, "Philip-pines!"

And the Filipina nuns exploded in joy, and some of them bent to their knees as he passed.

Now he looked at another little group and he shook his cane comically again and said, "Brah-SILL!"

And the Brazilians applauded and started to cry.

And the pope walked on, shuffling more quickly now, and approached an extraordi-nary-looking young man with coal-black hair, thick and cut so that it was standing straight up, looking like Pentecost hair. He was slim, Asian, dressed like a seminarian. He was looking dreamily, happily, his hands together in the attitude of prayer —

And the pope stopped, turned, and held his cane toward him.

"China!" he said.

And the young man, as if slain, slid to his knees, bent toward the floor, and went to kiss the pope's shoe.

And the pope caught him in an embrace as if to say, no, I am not your hero, you are my hero.

And from nowhere came to me an electric charge of thought: *I have just witnessed a future saint embrace a future cardinal of Beijing.*

My eyes filled with tears. The pope proceeded down the line. As he came closer, I tried to think of what to say. Of all he meant to me. But it was too exciting. There is no right thing to say when you meet a saint in the flesh, when you meet a giant who wants to shake your hand and keep going. And suddenly he was inches from me, to my left. I just wanted to touch him. He came closer and his frozen face was before me. One eye bigger than the other, and tearing. I touched his left hand with my hands. When later I thought of his face, I would think of the scene near the end of the Tom Hanks movie *Cast Away* in which he is floating on his raft at sea, and a giant whale rises from the deep and looks at him with an ancient eye.

I sort of curtsy-bowed, like an awkward person. And then as I held his hand, I leaned forward and kissed his thick old knuckles. I think I said, "Papa" or "Hello, papa." He looked at me, and pressed into my hand a soft brown plastic envelope. It was two inches square and bore an imprint of the papal seal. When I opened it later, I saw inexpensive white plastic rosary beads bearing a silver Christ on the cross, his body broken and ungainly. It is the Christ the pope carries at the top of his crozier, his long silver staff, when he enters the world.

I still have the picture of our meeting. I never saw anyone take it and was surprised to receive it in the mail from the cardinal's office. I look happy, transported. John Paul looks serious.

The last on our line was the Canadian heavy-metal rocker. When the pope came to him, the young man bowed and kissed his hand. He said, "I have written music for you." And he showed the pope a sheet of music, beautifully hand drawn, and it had a title like "A Song for John Paul II."

The pope looked at it and said, "You wrote?"

And the rocker, rocking, said, "Yes, for you."

The pope took it, walked a few feet away to where there was a big brown table, and signed the sheet music in a big flourish — Johannes Paulus II. He came back and gave it to the rocker.

And then he walked on, and out of the room.

There was silence again until it was broken softly by my rocker. "This is the greatest moment of my life," he said.

And I was wordless, for it is a great honor to be present at the greatest moment of someone's life.

And then we were ushered out. Some people were weeping and some were laughing. I was just lighter than air. I went into the streets of Rome, hailed a cab, told the driver the name of my hotel, and was still so excited I left my eyeglasses behind me on the seat.

But I remembered the rosary beads. Right now they are in my purse, in the next room.

A good thing happened with that rosary. For a year I kept it and showed it to people and thought to frame it with the picture. And then one day, in the middle of trouble in my life, I did with it what those who give you such things hope for you to do.

I said a Rosary. And then another.

But before that happened I had to be sort of knocked on the head with information I'd not been receiving, or been avoiding.

It was the summer of 2002. I was going through a trial in my life, or rather a series of serious and painful challenges. When troubles come, as Shakespeare said, they come not as "single spies" but "full battalions." I was entertaining an army. There were family pressures, work problems, frustrations of all sorts. The world had blown up ten months before, on 9/11. And someone I loved a great deal was ill.

I felt that all these things might capsize me. Always before I had sailed without sinking in whatever seas. I had always been able to steady my little boat. I had never felt before that a thing might capsize my life.

During that time I often thought of the pope and of how he felt each morning, waking up to a day in which he might never, ever, feel well.

At this time, a close friend sent me a videotape about how to pray. On its plastic cover was a picture of small blue and gray pebbles. They shined as if they were under water. I put the tape in its cover on the top of the TV set in my bedroom. I'd walk by it now and then and notice and think *pretty pebbles.*

I had a friend who often said Rosary novenas. That is, every day he said the Rosary, and with a specific cause and intent in mind, which he talked to God about. He took great joy in saying the Rosary. I didn't think I knew another adult who did that every day, and with joy. But then I remembered a friend, the mother of one of the kids at my son's school, who had told me ten years earlier that she said a Rosary every day while on the treadmill. I found the image comic. She was a glamorous and socially active young woman, and I didn't know she was "religious." I asked her what she got from doing that. She sort of looked away for a moment and then looked back at me. "All I can tell you is if I say a Rosary, the day works; and if I don't, nothing works."

This stayed in my mind.

My friend the man who was saying the Rosary novenas inspired me. I wanted to say one too. He gave me a book on the rosary to help jump-start me. It was *Rosary: Mysteries, Meditations, and the Telling of the Beads* by Kevin Orlin Johnson, a writer of depth and ease whose subject is Catholic belief and tradition.

I opened the book and read it quickly over a few days. It explained what saying the Rosary is, how it starts with rosary beads, a "circlet of beads punctuated with larger beads or with holy medals in a sort of necklace arrangement, usually with a shorter string of beads attached to it, ending in a cross or crucifix." No one has to have one, no one has to say one, but for "at least a dozen centuries most people in the Church have owned a rosary in one form or another."

They're not for ornament but for praying. They don't have any power in themselves. "Rosary beads are only a way of counting repetitions of vocal prayers, so you have to do something with them before you get any good out of them." But the repetitions — simple prayers, repeated — aren't the point of the devotion either. These vocal prayers are "an aid to meditative prayer, to raising your mind and heart to God by meditating on the life of Jesus and Mary." These meditations are what constitute "the Rosary."

Clear enough. I liked reading this: "The immense spiritual, emotional, and even intellectual benefits of meditative prayer are the reason that so many millions of people pray the Rosary regularly — even daily. The Rosary works; the graces drawn down by this form of meditative prayer answer all petitions and supply all necessities . . ."

Well, I had plenty of petitions and needs.

All of this was interesting, but for some reason the part that was most striking to me was the explanation of the history. The Rosary started and began as a tradition *not* because the church hierarchy invented or ordained it, and *not* because priests advised it. It was a peoples' prayer. Lay members of the church came up with it, loved it, and spread it.

In the first centuries after Christ, a number of those who had heard his word and been converted to follow him retreated to the wilderness, turning the center of their lives to prayer. They would listen to their heartbeats and silently say, as they breathed in, "Jesus Christ, Son of God." As they breathed out they would silently say, "Have mercy on us."

Here is Johnson: "By repeating this or some similar prayer over and over again, they would relax their own wills, absorb themselves in this act of merciful prayer for all Mankind, and become immersed in an awareness of the presence of God."

The point was not to empty themselves out but open themselves up to God's grace.

So this, the saying of what came to be

known as the Jesus Prayer, is how the Rosary in effect began.

But not every Christian could live like a mystic monk in the desert. Others are called to other work, to build families and create community and embrace professions. And they wanted to take up this form of prayer too. So they began to say a certain number of vocal prayers each day, before or after they went on to work and the cares of the day. And these Christians began to count their prayers and mark them off with pebbles after each was done.

Johnson, on an early Christian mystic named Paul the Hermit: "Paul would pick up three hundred pebbles every morning and put them in his pocket (whatever Paul wore, it evidently had pockets) and throw one away each time he had repeated his prayer. As the centuries rolled on, monks and nuns continued to pray in this way even when they lived in large communities, which, being usually in the wilderness, had plenty of pebbles available."

And that was how they counted the prayers they'd vowed to say.

This was so interesting to me. A prayer itself seems so special, and yet a pebble is so common. And yet you can in effect build these common things together into something special, and even towering.

So I was thinking about pebbles — the pebbles on the cover of the videotape, the pebbles in the Kevin Orlin Johnson book, the pebbles I saw on Jones Beach when I went out that summer to see friends.

I thought a lot.

I just didn't say any Rosaries.

I find this to be true of my spiritual life, and maybe it applies to yours as well: I think about things more than I do them; I ponder what seems their goodness more than I perform them. As if my thought alone were enough. But a thought alone isn't quite enough; it's an impulse and not a commitment, a passing thing that doesn't take root unless you plant it and make it grow.

So I just thought about all this. And was very glad other people were saying Rosaries, and when I met them, I always asked that they pray for me.

Meanwhile, the problems I was having were growing more urgent. And I would talk to God about them. But I didn't say the Rosary.

And then I believe I was told to do it.

This is what happened:

I got up one sunny morning and did

what I always do: went to the kitchen and made coffee in a white plastic Braun coffeemaker. I don't have a cup of coffee in the morning — I have a glass of coffee, because it's bigger. I use one of those heavy tumblers you'd get at a hardware or department store, made by the Duralex company. So every morning I pour the coffee into the tumbler and then add milk and go do whatever I'm doing.

That morning as I dreamily poured the coffee I was thinking that I ought to pray more. I ought to say a morning prayer. I should —

Kaboom!

An explosion.

I was so surprised I couldn't register what had happened.

The glass I was pouring the coffee into no longer existed. It had exploded into little pieces that were scattered all over the floor and counter, all the way over to the sink.

I just stood there with the Braun coffeepot in my hand.

"What was that?" called my son, from his bedroom.

"My glass of coffee exploded," I said.

"It sounded like a big piggy bank exploded," he said.

I put down the coffeepot and looked at the mess. There was coffee all over, all the way up the cupboard, on the refrigerator and on the ceiling. There was coffee all over the front of my white T-shirt. And this is the thing: My first thought was that the coffee must have been unusually hot, and maybe the tumbler had had a crack or had just been hit with the heat in the wrong way, and so it had broken.

But the coffee wasn't hot. I could feel it on my body. The front of my T-shirt was soaked with it. It was lukewarm. In fact, when it sort of exploded on me, it felt good. It felt warming.

And what happened didn't strike me as upsetting. It felt . . . peaceful.

This was all perplexing, but not disturbing. It seemed interesting, like a puzzle.

I picked up a piece of glass. It was about an eighth of an inch long and wide. I picked up another and another. Then, for no reason, I picked up all of them. There were hundreds. They were small and smooth. They weren't jagged. None of them were big; but for a few, they were all pretty much the same size. You could roll them in your hand. I did roll them in my hand. They were as smooth as pebbles.

So I gathered them up and put them in a

paper towel, and then I rinsed them off in the sink in the towel and put them on the windowsill to dry. Then I put them in a pretty crystal wineglass. As I write, they are on the windowsill beyond my computer.

You wonder why I kept them.

The reason is I don't think it was a weak or cracked glass. I feel that it was God talking to me. He was saying: Pebbles!

He was saying: I'm trying to get your attention here!

He was saying: There is explosive power in the pebbles.

He was saying: There is explosive power in what appear to be *mere* pebbles. There is explosive power in the Rosary, for instance. And I want you to know this.

I don't know how long it took me to figure this all out, but I think it was quick. I remember thinking, when I realized the coffee all over my shirt and me was warm and not hot, and felt good and not burning: *This feels like a little miracle.*

I think you know where this is going.

I began to say the Rosary, and for a while I did it every day. I had a few rosaries I'd bought over the years because I thought they were so pretty. But I didn't use them.

And now suddenly I was, and I found out what my friend had told me, the one who said it every morning on her treadmill: Everything turned out fine when I said these prayers. I also said a Rosary novena, and here's a stupid thing: I can't remember exactly what I was asking for. But I must have asked for a lot because I got a lot.

What I got was not so much gifts and wishes come true but a feeling of peace. I got peace itself, actually. And when you have peace, you can be strong; and when you are strong, you can get through what you have to get through, and not with exhaustion and frown marks and slumped shoulders but with relative happiness, and humor, and sometimes even gaiety.

I loved saying my Rosary. I attempted once to do it with a friend who tried every day to say the Rosary while walking along the streets of Manhattan. This struck me as a very happy thing to do but when we did it, I was distracted by the fact that we perhaps looked insane. We'd walk along saying our prayers, and it seemed obvious that we looked like two ladies with their heads down mumbling to themselves. Sometimes I tried it on my own, intending to walk along and pray silently, but I sometimes started praying out loud, and then I was a lone lady mumbling to herself. (In the spring of 2003, I had dinner with the woman who walks along saying the Rosary, and she told me that technology had made everything easier. How, I asked. "With cell phones and earpieces half the people on the sidewalks of New York look like they're talking to themselves. I fit right in now.")

What I learned to love most was saying the Rosary on the subway when I was going into Manhattan from Brooklyn. I would bring the rosary the pope had given me because it was the only one I had in a little case, so I'd throw the case in my pocket and jump the number 4 or 5 uptown. All of the amazing and highly individualized people down there in the subway would be going about their business and talking to one another and sometimes arguing with one another, and I'd just be sitting there, standing there, saying my Rosary and praying for all of us and everyone. And wherever I went, I feel, I felt, there was peace. This was surprising. Once, when I was on the subway downtown, going home from some meeting in the city, it was crowded and it was tense for some reason — maybe we'd been caught in a stall between stops — and a big tall woman with a Jamaican accent who appeared to be high on drugs got into a fight with a man whose block she threatened to knock off. I liked her; she seemed strong and intelligent and passionate, but she was pushing the guy around verbally and growing all the more insistent and nearing the edge of rage because she experienced herself to be the person who was being pushed around. I continued to say my prayers but directed them in my mind toward the woman; and in time she calmed down, after the intervention of a diplomatic passenger, so fisticuffs were averted. Another time, a creepy man was bothering a young woman who was being polite to him, but he was scaring her, so I prayed on him and he got off at the next stop. Obviously this has nothing to do with my power, because I don't have power. But all prayers are a request — at the very least they mean "Please hear me" — and when you turn them to peace, there's a greater chance peace will occur.

The person I cared about who was ill entered the process of being healed, and is now healed, which is beautiful to see.

Naturally — this is so amazing about human beings, and I am naturally embarrassed to tell you this part — I kept saying the Rosary for a year or two and then stopped and went on to other things. This is like being on a successful vitamin regimen that makes you completely healthy and happy, and so you tell all your friends and advise them to do it — and then you stop taking the vitamins yourself. We are perverse. But I'm thinking this chapter might remind me of what I know, and turn me around.

I should get back to the pope, to John Paul. Because he had put in my hand the rosary beads I used on the subway, I began to associate him with saying the Rosary.

And yet it was startling to me when he did something in the twenty-fourth year of his reign that struck others as wholly off the point, and me as wholly on and to the point.

He changed the Rosary. This was kind of an amazing decision. No one could remember the last time a pope changed the Rosary. It would have been hundreds of years. It could have been a millennium.

But here it was, October 2002, and John Paul II decided to add to the litany of the Rosary what he called the Luminous Mysteries.

Now as I said earlier, the point and purpose of the Rosary is not to recite rote prayers but to repeat prayers you know by heart — the Hail Mary, the Lord's Prayer — as you contemplate a mystery of Christianity. A mystery in this context being an important event whose entire meaning you won't fully understand in this world.

For roughly nine hundred years there have been three groups of mysteries included in the Rosary: the Joyous Mysteries (Christ enters the world), the Sorrowful Mysteries (Christ is abused and put to death), and the Glorious Mysteries (Christ and Heaven). What John Paul did was to add a new set of mysteries, the Luminous Mysteries, which encompassed Christ's ministry and teachings.

The most startling thing about the pope's announcement was that the new mysteries didn't seem so much an addition to a tradition as the logical filling of a gap. The new mysteries seemed like something that might originally have been part of the Rosary tradition but had somehow been lost along the way. The Joyful Mysteries, for instance, end with Christ being found, at age twelve, in the temple, where he'd been teaching the elders. The Sorrowful Mysteries start with Christ suffering in Gethsemane the night before his death. It was odd to contemplate the Joyfuls one day and then jump, on the next, to the Sorrowfuls, with nothing in between. Something was missing. That would be the Luminous Mysteries, which offer for contemplation what Christ did and said as an adult, which is what the pope added.

So it seemed organic, natural. But why did John Paul rewrite the Rosary after it had existed in a codified form for hundreds of years? "He is making a statement at the end of his life about what's important to him," said Father C. J. McCloskey, of Washington's Catholic Information Center, when I called him to ask why the pope would do such an unusual thing. "By adding these mysteries he is saying, 'This is another invitation to look closely at the life of Christ, to contemplate and meditate.' "

"To think," I offered.

"Not to think," he said. "To let the life of Christ sink into you."

Arthur J. Hughes, a history professor at St. Francis College, of Brooklyn, New York, talked to me about the Luminous Mysteries — and he spoke with excitement even a year after they were introduced — "John Paul gave us the mysteries that belong to us, to the people, to the life we live.

The Host, the wedding at Cana — this is the life of the people." Not solely the life of Christ, but the life of the people. "This pope's a real thinker," he said. "And he's the best we've had in my lifetime."

The timing of the pope's decision and announcement seemed interesting. The Rosary is by long tradition a prayer for peace in the world. In the Church-sanctioned visitations of Mary — there have been more reported visions in the past 150 years than in all the previous centuries combined — the Blessed Mother has asked in almost all cases that the Rosary be said for peace. And the day he made the announcement, the pope dedicated the entire coming year to the Rosary. He did it in a way that was embracing of other Christian traditions, asserting that the Rosary is "Christocentric," a way of thinking about Jesus through and with the mother who gave him life and witnessed his living it. This was an invitation to all Christians to take a new look at the old devotion, one that some Protestants have seen as unhappily Marycentric in the past.

In his announcement, John Paul used the words *luminous* or *light* twenty-nine times, which reminded me of the prophecies of Saint Malachi, the mystic of the

161

Middle Ages who had named each future pope with a phrase and who referred to John Paul's pontificate with the words, "Of the Labors of the Sun." The most luminous star, the bringer of light to the world.

I want to say a few words too on the difficulty of contemplation, which is something I wrestled with. The pope said in his letter that he sensed a great hunger in the world for meditation, and made clear he meant to help feed it in part with the offering of the new mysteries. When I was a new Rosary sayer, I was struck by the difficulties of meditating and contemplating, and I found some helpful counsel in the pope's letter.

I did not know how to meditate when I began saying the Rosary. So I'd just begin by imagining particular scenes in my mind. In the first Joyful Mystery, for instance, the angel Gabriel comes to a girl of perhaps fourteen or sixteen and announces that she is to become the mother of God. She replies, Yes, what the Lord wants is what should be done. This scene is described in Saint Luke's Gospel. So I'd try to imagine it. But then the phone would ring and I would listen to see if the message came on, or an ambulance would go by, and suddenly I would find myself daydreaming. I'd be wondering why Mary is never reported to have fainted or run away when an angel walked into her garden and started talking to her. Maybe she'd been seeing angels for years. Maybe she thought they were her playmates when she was a child. Maybe they were commonplace to her, and that's part of the reason she seems to have moved through life with unbroken serenity.

The third Joyful Mystery is the birth of Christ in a manger. It's not hard to imagine this; it's hard to control one's imaginings. You'd imagine the trek to the manger, the sounds coming from the eating area of the inn the Holy Family had just passed, a bawdy joke and laughter as they trudged by. And then you'd wonder if Mary was in pain; did she weep him into the world? She was barely more than a child herself, with a young husband and no help, just the two of them in the cold in a hut on a hill . . . And when the child was born, did he cry aloud with a great wail, and did the cry enter the universe, and did it become a sound wave of unusual or significant density? Is it still out there radiating its way out into the stars, and did *Voyager 2* bump into it, and did it jostle its cameras and change what it saw?

Did someone unrecorded by history see a light in the hut on the hill the night Christ was born, and come to help Mary and Joseph? Maybe there was an old woman with moles and wens and a sharply bent nose, a woman almost comically ugly, like a witch in a child's Halloween book. Maybe she lived in isolation, never left her own little hovel, but that night felt called to assist, tugged by some wonder that pierced her estrangement. Maybe she helped with the birth, and hers was the first face he saw. Maybe her outer appearance was an expression of the inner wounds he came to heal. Maybe she wrapped him in rags; maybe she bent down, breathed him in, her face bathed by the mist of a rough birth on a frosty night. Maybe when she returned home, she was beautiful. But no one knew because she never left her hut again. Even she didn't know she'd been made lovely. No, maybe she went out the next day, the first time she'd gone out in the day in thirty years, and she went by a booth in the market and saw a looking glass and was stunned . . .

You see the problem. I found it difficult to concentrate on what we believe we know. I still do. I have wondered if we don't, so many of us, enjoy making amusing filigrees around the truth, not to enhance it but to avoid it. I concentrate on the first Sorrowful Mystery, Christ in the night in the garden of Gethsemane. He was suffering, in deep anguish. Maybe . . . Maybe he was thinking that in spite of the pain to which he was about to be subjected, in spite of his self-sacrifice, the world was going to continue to be a miserable place. Maybe the evil one sneaked into his mind and taunted him with a film of the future — Thomas More being put to death as a Christian by Christians, Edmund Campion and John Fisher the same. The Inquisition, the Holocaust, cardinals of the church who would be incapable of showing compassion for the families of children abused by priests. Maybe all of that is what made him sweat blood. And he must have loved life. *He must have been in love with life on earth.* He must have wanted to grow old. He knew of heaven and yet he wanted to stay here. Did he love the taste of bread, the sound of the animals on the hills? He must have liked being a carpenter's apprentice. In woodwork you can see the results of your labor, you can touch it, you can feel its smooth finish. Maybe he once made a chair. Maybe no one knows but a chair made by Christ is in the Museum of Natural History in Manhattan right now, in a case with a card that reads, CHILD'S CHAIR, CIRCA 100 B.C.E. Maybe there's a guard in the museum who's in love with a girl on the third floor. Maybe they met in front of the case with the chair. Maybe . . .

You see where I am. I am daydreaming, not meditating.

But here was the pope in the letter on the rosary: to announce each mystery as you begin to pray, to focus on it, is "to open up a scenario." The words you are saying direct "the imagination and the mind" toward a particular "episode." In Catholic spirituality, "visual and imaginative elements" help in "concentrating the mind."

The pope cautioned that the process is "nourished by silence." Yes. "One drawback of a society dominated by technology and the mass media is the fact that silence becomes increasingly difficult to achieve." Don't we know it. "You must try to both be silent, and find a quiet place to let thoughts come in and sit down." So try not to be near the phone and the siren, open your mind to the images and words with which you are feeding it, let your imagination go, as long as where it goes is a good place to be. This seemed not only like good advice, but also advice I especially needed.

This is unconnected, but to me connected because at the moment I can't stop thinking about Christ and his desire to live. What I think of when I think about it is the composer and performer Warren Zevon. Like the pope, he was a philosopher, though I don't suppose he would have thought of himself that way. He said something very true about life on earth though, and it is worth more than gold and diamonds.

When he was dying of lung cancer, in the autumn of 2002, Zevon did an hour-long interview with David Letterman. Letterman asked, "From your perspective now, do you know something about life and death that maybe I don't know?" And Zevon famously replied, "I know how much you're supposed to enjoy every sandwich."

He knew how wonderful and delicious the smallest parts of daily life are. He knew how wonderful and delicious a day in your life, or an hour of that day, or this minute is.

We're lucky to be here. And now when I

think of friends and family and those I love, or those I'm just getting to know, I think, "He knows how good the sandwich is." Or "She doesn't know how good the sandwich is yet." But it's good to know. More fun too.

CHAPTER EIGHT

Men at Work

John Paul was inspiring in part because when he spoke of man his words shined with respect. He always made clear in his writings and public statements his conviction that God loves — truly loves — mankind.

He believed in a very personal way that man was created in the image of God. That isn't just a famous phrase, "made in the image of God." It means something concrete and factual. To John Paul it meant God actually made human beings to be *like* him — similar to him or reflective of him, or of an aspect or aspects of him. And God did this, the pope taught, in part because he wanted man to be an object of his love, to be his friend. You don't want your friends to be slaves, you want them to be free, and to fully choose you. God didn't build us, the pope has said, to be frightened and obsequious; he built us to have and love freedom, and to use that freedom to choose and accept his love, and love him back.

If God, the creator of all things, built

man to be like him, then it follows, the pope asserts, that he also built man to create — to bring into being, to discover, to break through in a continuing quest for artistic and scientific and intellectual and moral truth. We are called to build. We are called to expand, imagine, originate, give rise to.

One day when we were speaking about the pope, the writer Michael Novak mentioned that he had been thinking about religion and iconography. When you think of Catholic iconography, he said, you might think of portraits of the saints. They are usually looking up, their eyes fixed on something luminous from above. However, in Islam, he noted, the image that comes to your mind might be a man on his knees on a prayer rug, eyes shut or fixed downward, forehead to the carpet. The subjects of these portraits are worshipping, honoring, but the emphasis is on obeisance — the idea of "I'm nothing; you are everything." This does not reflect the reaching and aspirational nature of Christianity. The saints looking upward longingly and seeing something does.

Novak was saying that the pope's message was in part: You are *not* nothing; you are a great deal. God made you in his image, and he calls you to be like him. And so you must walk forward into the world each day with confidence and humility. This reminded me of what a woman in Bible study said once. "Walk with pride, for you are the daughter of a king."

Novak's comments seemed connected in my mind to the pope's ideas about how man is called, like God, to create. John Paul II has written that part of how we create each day is through the work we do. Work can be seen as a looking up. "To work is to pray," as they used to say.

I am a worker — are you? I have built much of my life and, I suppose, what is called self-image on the work I do and the contribution that I attempt to make professionally. This matters to me, as it matters to many Americans — most of us, really. We're the great Work Nation.

John Paul's encyclical "Laborem Exercens," "On Human Work," is essentially a gospel of work. In work, he says, we are called "to imitate God." Through work we take part in "the very action of the Creator of the universe." Our work is a vocation to which we have been called from the beginning of time. In fact, John Paul wrote, when we work, we are partaking in and

171

joining with God's ongoing creation of the world.

We know this in part, the pope asserts, because God made Christ a worker, an itinerant preacher, a carpenter whose earthly father was also a workingman, a carpenter.

The pope writes that work speaks not only of what we produce, it speaks also of who we are; in fact, it can help us become who we are. Work helps us achieve "fulfillment as a human being." It reflects our human dignity.

The pope was not an economist, but he sometimes made reference to particular economic systems. He did not oppose free market activities, but he made it clear that such activities must be intensely humane. He states in "Laborem Exercens" that the worker is always more important than mere capital, that work is not to be understood in some abstract economic model as simply being part of an economic purpose or program. Work must be informed by fair, generous, and just treatment of the worker.

The pope speaks too of unions, which he put forward as organizations that in themselves can help advance man's rights. Support of unions and trade unions is part of church tradition, but the pope's stand on them was stirringly expressed. Unions are "movements of solidarity" that must exist not only to advance improved worker conditions but also to assert the "humanity" of the worker and his place in "the development of the Kingdom of God." (The pope issued his encyclical on work in September 1983, when the Polish freedom union Solidarity was holding its first annual congress, in Gdansk, Poland. The Soviet Union responded to the congress by launching what it called "training exercises" in the Baltic, which included, in case anyone didn't get the point, landing Soviet troops on the coasts of Lithuania and Latvia. The pope wanted Solidarity, and the Soviets, to know exactly whose side he was on, and whom he was pulling for.)

The encyclical insists on the right to private property, but at the same time, it asserts what George Weigel calls "a social mortgage" on it. Property is part of what makes creativity possible, but the owner must see to it that that creativity is used for the general good of man.

I read the pope on work early in the 1990s, read what he said of its dignity and deeper meaning, and it helped me to think in a new way of the meaning (as opposed to, say, the gain or the loss, the drawbacks and rewards) of what I do. Of what *we* do.

More than twenty years have passed since John Paul wrote his encyclical. But if you read it again now, it seems fresher and more pertinent than it did even then. At that time, the big issue that overlay everything was communism and its chronic and inherent abuse of workers, versus capitalism and its abuses, which were less prevalent but still present.

Now, twenty years later, the topic that seems to overlay everything is who you are as a worker, and what your work means.

The pope's words on the moral dimension of labor are needed now more than ever — at least for those of us in the West — because we in the affluent democracies have become confused about the meaning of work, or have perhaps lost some of its meaning, in part perhaps because of the very rewards we receive for our work. For so many in our society the rewards are largely material, and for some they are outsized. It is hard to imagine how, if you get a bonus of ten million dollars on Wall Street just for doing your job each day, it would not tend to be individually destabilizing, at least to some degree.

I think of three scenes of work in the 1990s and the 2000s.

It is a spring day in the early 1990s, and I am talking with the head of a mighty American corporation. We're in his window-lined office, high in midtown Manhattan. The view — silver skyscrapers stacked one against another, dense, fine lined, sparkling in the sun — is so perfect, so theatrical, it's like a scrim, like a fake backdrop for a 1930s movie about people in tuxes and tails. Edward Everett Horton could shake his cocktail shaker here; Fred and Ginger could banter on the phone.

The CEO tells me it is "annual report time" and he is looking forward to reading the reports of his competitors.

Why? I asked. I wondered what he looks for specifically when he reads the reports of the competition.

He said he always flipped to the back to see what the other CEOs got as part of their deal — corporate jets, private helicopters, whatever. "We all do that," he said. "We all want to see who has what."

He was a talented and exceptional man, and I thought afterward that he might, in an odd way, be telling me this about him-self so I wouldn't be unduly impressed by him. But what I thought was: *It must be hard for him to keep some simple things in mind each day as he works.* Such as this: A job creates a livelihood, a livelihood cre-ates a family, a family creates civilization. Ultimately, he was in the civilization-pro-ducing business. Did he know it? Did it give him joy? Did he understand that that was probably why he was there?

I thought: *This man creates the jobs that create the world in which we live. And yet he can't help it, his mind is on the jet.*

Second scene: I am talking to a cele-brated veteran of Wall Street and big busi-ness. The WorldCom story had broken that day, and he told me about it. He had a look I saw more and more often in the 1990s, a kind of facelift look, but it doesn't involve a facelift. It's like this: The face blanches and goes blank, and the eyes go up slightly as if the hairline had been yanked back. He looked scalped by history.

For years, he said, he had been giving the same speech throughout Europe on why they should invest in America. We have the great unrigged game, he'd tell them, we have oversight and regulation, we're the great stable democracy with reliable, responsible capitalism. "I can't give that speech anymore," he said.

Third scene: It is the midnineties, a spring afternoon, and I am crossing a broad Manhattan avenue. I think it was Third, it may have been Lexington. I was doing errands. Soon I would pick up my son at school. I began to cross the avenue with the light, but halfway across I saw it switch to yellow. I picked up my pace. From the corner of my eye I saw, then heard, the car. Bright black Mercedes, high gloss, brand-new. The man at the wheel — dark haired, in his thirties, was gunning the motor. *Vroom, vroom.* He drummed his fingers impatiently on the steering wheel. The light turned red. He *vroomed* forward. I sprinted the last few steps toward the sidewalk. He sped by so close that as he passed, the wind made my skirt move. I realized: *If I hadn't sprinted, that guy would have hit me.*

I thought: *He's a bright young Wall Street titan, a bonus bum.* For a moment I hated him.

Something has been wrong with — what shall we call it? — Wall Street, Big Business, Big Money. Something has been wrong with it for a long time. Those who invested in and placed faith in companies like Global Crossing, Enron, Tyco, or WorldCom were cheated and fooled by individuals whose selfishness seemed so outsized, so huge, that it seems less human and flawed than weird and puzzling. Did they think they would get away with accounting scams forever? Did they think it was okay?

I began to read Michael Novak. Twenty years ago this summer he published *The Spirit of Democratic Capitalism*, a stunning book marked by clarity of expression and originality of thought. But it was also, I realized as I read, a response to the pope's encyclical on work, or rather an elaboration on it.

Novak says there is one great reason that capitalism is good: Of all the systems devised by man, it is the one most likely to lift the poor out of poverty. But capitalism cannot exist in a void. Capitalism requires an underlying moral edifice. Without it nothing works; with it, all is possible. That edifice includes people who have an appreciation for and understanding of the human person; it requires a knowledge that business can contribute to community and family; it requires "a sense of sin," a sense of right and wrong, and an appreciation that the unexpected happens, that things take surprising turns in life.

Mr. Novak was speaking, he knew, to an international academic and intellectual community that, in the 1980s, felt toward capitalism a generalized contempt. Capitalism was selfish, exploitative, unequal, imperialistic. He himself had been a socialist and knew the critiques, but he had come to see capitalism in a new way.

Capitalism, like nature, wants to increase itself, wants to grow and create, and as it does, it produces more — more goods, more services, more "liberation," more creativity, more opportunity, more possibilities, more unanticipated ferment, movement, action.

So capitalism was to Mr. Novak a public good, and he addressed its subtler critics. What of "the corruption of affluence," the idea that although it is moral discipline that builds and creates success, success tends in time to corrupt and corrode moral discipline? Dad made money with his guts; you spend it at your leisure. The result, goes this thinking, is an ethos of self-indulgence, greed, narcissism.

Mr. Novak answers by quoting the philosopher Jacques Maritain, who once observed that affluence, in fact, inspires us to look beyond the material for meaning in our lives. "It's exactly because people have bread that they realize you can't live by bread alone." In a paradoxical way, says Mr. Novak, the more materially comfortable a society becomes, the more spiritual it is able to become, "its hungers more markedly transcendent."

Right now Mr. Novak certainly seems right about American society in general. We have not become worse people with the affluence of the past twenty years, and have arguably become better in some interesting ways. (Forty years ago, men in the New York City borough of Queens ignored the screams of a waitress named Kitty Genovese as she was stabbed to death in an apartment building parking lot. Today men of Queens are famous for strapping seventy pounds of gear on their backs and charging into the Twin Towers.)

But it appears that the leaders of business, of Wall Street, of big accounting have, many of them, become worse with affluence. I know a man of celebrated rectitude who, if he returned to the Wall Street of his youth, would no doubt be welcomed back with cheers and derided behind his back as a sissy. He wouldn't dream of cooking the books. He wouldn't dream of calling costs profits. He would never fit in.

Mr. Novak famously sees business as a vocation, a deeply serious one. Business to him is a stage, a platform on which men and women can each day take actions that are either ethical or unethical, helpful or not. When their actions are marked by high moral principle, they heighten their calling — they are suddenly not just "in business" but part of a noble endeavor that adds to the sum total of human joy and progress. The work they do makes connections between people, forges community, spreads wealth, sets an example, creates a template, offers inspiration. The work they do changes the world. And in doing this work, they strengthen the ground on which democracy and economic freedom stand. "The calling of business is to support the reality and reputation of capitalism," says Mr. Novak, "and not undermine [it]."

Edward Younkins, of the Acton Institute, has distilled Mr. Novak's philosophy into Seven Great Responsibilities for Corporations: Satisfy customers with good services of real value; make a reasonable return to investors; create new wealth; create new jobs; defeat cynicism and envy by demonstrating internally that talent and hard work will and can be rewarded; promote inventiveness, ingenuity, and creativity; diversify the interests of the republic.

John Paul was a European. He came of age during fascism and lived as an adult under communism. His view of economic freedom was largely a European one heavily influenced by his era: The state isn't all bad and isn't all good, some kind of combined socialist-capitalist system is probably to be desired. The poor must always be cared for, the ill taken in, healed, or comforted. Always he is more interested in the human person, including the individual as worker. I was interested to hear what he said of Michael Novak's response to his encyclical when it first came out twenty years ago. John Paul read it, and then told friends, "This is a good book."

What about work in the arts? What about artists? It might seem odd that a pope would have devoted a great amount of time to pondering the role of the artist in society, but in this case it is not. John Paul as a student thought he might become an actor; he appeared in local productions in college and the seminary, and it was clear he had a gift. He wrote plays as a young man, and felt called to playwriting. And he remained throughout his life a poet.

In 1999, John Paul wrote a long letter to the artists of the world. I read it two years later, after September 11, 2001, when I had come to see my work as more than a way of taking part in the world and earning my living. Writing about the human drama that surrounded the event — the valor of the firemen, and how none walk through fire but for love; the pain and anguish of those who lost friends and family members; the brave search of so many for the meaning of the event; the honest search for lessons and understanding — writing about this in the year after 9/11, I began to experience another dimension in my own work, another reason for doing it. I wanted to serve. I wanted to honor. I wanted to see in a new way and speak of our connectedness. And I wanted to be truthful, to point out what I believed I saw: a return on the part of the culture to admiration for an old style of masculinity, the kind that takes responsibility and saves others, and a renewed cultural sense in my beloved New York that religion is not something we should hold utterly private or be mildly embarrassed about, but rather something we can hold high, not with aggression or pride but with love and gratitude. Well, I have had few times in my professional life when I could feel that what I was doing was attempting something like art, something like painting, with the portrait painter's fierce desire to make it true and capture the subject. And so at that time I read the pope's letter.

A glimmer of God's work at the dawn of Creation can be seen in the eyes of an artist, the pope asserts. Artists are captivated by the hidden power of sounds and words, colors and shapes. This, he says, is both an echo of Creation and also God's way of associating you, as a person, with his Creation. "The opening pages of the Bible present God as a kind of exemplar of everyone who produces a work"; the "human craftsman" mirrors the Creator.

In producing a work and expressing themselves, John Paul says, artists' work becomes "a unique disclosure of their own being." In shaping a masterpiece, "the artist not only summons his work into being, but also in some way reveals his own personality by means of it." Art is thus an "exceptional mode of expression for spiritual growth." Because the artist communicates with his fellow men, the history of art is "not only a story of works produced but also a story of men and women."

But the artist's vocation is in the service of beauty. When God looked at what he'd made, he saw not only that it was good but that it was beautiful. "In a certain sense, beauty is the visible form of the good." And all art is a constant striving. "Every genuine artistic intuition goes beyond what the senses perceive." The artistic intuition springs from the human soul and grasps, if only fleetingly and imperfectly, "the mysterious unity of things." All artists experience the gap between what they do and the "perfection of the beauty glimpsed in the ardor of the creative moment." What an artist manages to express in a painting or a creation is no more than "a glimmer" of "splendor."

Art is hard. The true artist nears God in his work, is "overwhelmed," and "can only stammer in reply." But true artists know this. They know, as Saint Paul said, "God does not dwell in shrines made of human hands." And yet their perseverance is an act of faith: The closer the artist comes to beauty, the closer he comes to Christ. To journey toward truth is to journey toward God. In the murk is the mystery, and in the mystery is all Creation, and the Creator.

★ ★ ★

I would read this and ponder. In 2004, I had a conversation with an artist who'd been doing the same thing. He is the actor Jim Caviezel, who portrayed Jesus in *The Passion of the Christ*. I spoke to him by phone when he was in Rome, about to meet John Paul. *The Passion* had just opened, with all its surrounding drama. Some in the Vatican had attempted to help the film when it came under the fire of charges that it was anti-Semitic. The pope was shown the film and was quoted as saying, by those who were there, "It is as it was." The meaning of that statement seemed to be that the film was not vicious and hateful but an attempt to artistically render the truth. The quote was reported to me by the film's producer, who had reason to want it disseminated. I contacted the pope's press spokesman, Dr. Navarro-Valls, and told him what I had been told, repeating to him the exact words I was told the pope had said. He gave me permission to report it. I did, as did others. But within days the Vatican came to fear that it had become embroiled in a great controversy, one that was showing up on page one of the *New York Times*. And Dr. Navarro-Valls told a reporter he had never given anyone permission to use such a quote. He also suggested I had invented our e-mail correspondence. This put me on the spot, to say the least. I went to the *Wall Street Journal* with Dr. Navarro-Valls's e-mail to me. We traced it back to the Vatican, and to the press office. I duly reported this. Dr. Navarro-Valls had no response.

It was quite a mess, with the *Times* criticizing me on one hand as a supporter of anti-Semitic art, and the Vatican attacking my integrity. I think I will never forget, in the middle of the drama, going to a book party for a friend in Manhattan. There I bumped into the gossip columnist Liz Smith, in a circle of sophisticated New Yorkers. "Well, you're in the fire," she teased. I laughed and agreed. Then I said, "I am either being misled and abused by cynical Hollywood producers or by the Vatican of my great faith. Which do you think it is?" "The Vatican," they all replied, with confidence. And we laughed, because it was a surprising thing to think, and yet it is what appeared to be true.

Soon the Vatican, embarrassed by its awkward maneuvers — other reporters had come forward with their own experiences of being told of the pope's quote — decided to make up by having the star of the movie in to see John Paul. His blessing, they no doubt thought, would make clear once and for all the pope's support of the film.

Jim Caviezel, an ardent Catholic and gifted actor, was thrilled to meet the man he told me was his hero. By phone, after the meeting, he spoke of the recent controversy, thanked me for my stand, said he would be grateful if I could report what had transpired between him and John Paul. What he wanted to tell me was this: On seeing the pope and taking his hand, he found himself thinking of John Paul's letter to the artists of the world. Caviezel told me, "I read it several times when I was a young actor. It was very important to me. It came out, and I remember what he said is that part of the truth, right, is accepting — you can't just write about darkness and say, 'This is the way it is,' because light always comes through. It must. If you went into a forty-thousand-foot warehouse, even if you just light a match, the match pierces the darkness. It pierces even in the vast amount of darkness. As I see it, the movie is a light, it is a match. So the first thing I began to talk about was his letter to the artists. I told him it gave me great strength in my life and my career. I thanked him. I said, 'Thank you.' The pope . . . this is a very holy man. He's seen the Nazis and the communists [and there were] people he knew that understand what a regime is like and what they do, and how they can take your freedom from you. He's seen it. This is the pope from Fatima. I think the guy's a mystic. He's a saint. I'm not impressed by celebrity — that word is bad when you're standing in front of a saint. But something moved me. I know he is a saint."

Caviezel asked for the pope's blessing for himself, his work, and his family. He spoke to John Paul of *The Passion* itself, of artistic decisions that had been made in its filming. Caviezel told me, "I always knew if it's gonna rock, you have to have Mary [prominent in the film's story]. There are different Christian traditions and ways and views, but let the Holy Spirit do his work; I'm not denying the mother. What her son said on the cross, 'Mother behold your son; son behold your mother' — it's one of the seven things Jesus said on the cross. He said it. You can't leave it out, so if you include it, you have to develop it; you have to tell the story, to show it. He was giving his mother to the world. He gave his mother to John, to the world."

Caviezel told John Paul that he had noticed the pope had "boldly put the M on your crest." Caveizel told the pope, "She is the one I think who made the movie for her son." "I told [the pope], 'Your statement, your example.' She knew the great pain. We put her son to death for saying 'Be a good person.' Well, he told the truth. The truth cuts like a sword. That's the sword right there, 'Be a good person.' "

Caviezel told me, "In the world, we make good as evil and evil as good. But here's a guy [the pope] who doesn't do that. He carries a lot of crosses. I don't know how he functions. And there's politics everywhere — everywhere. But the church will survive. It'll be here when we're dust."

And then Caviezel spoke to me as an artist who had just been through a grueling artistic endeavor.

"When this whole thing began — I met one day with Mel [Gibson], and we're talking about other roles, and then stories in the Bible, and he's looking at me. And I said, 'You want me to play Jesus, don't you?' And he said, 'Yeah.'

"Your life builds up to things. When you're asked a question, when the whole history of your life comes to that moment

— 'You want me to play Christ, don't you?'
— God gives you a grace inside your heart that says, 'Look, this is where I need you.' One of the great saints — I read her — is Maria de Agreda, a mystic. She wrote that Mary said, 'If you truly follow my son, scandal will follow you all your life.' But okay — if they persecute you, they persecuted [Christ] first.

"Miraculous things have happened. I was hit by lightning [during the filming of a crucifixion scene]. It was the one day I didn't have communion. We always had Mass and I always received communion but on that one day the priest ran out of Hosts. I was up there on the cross and I was hit, and we knew I was going to be hit — we could see [the lightning] coming. And the eyes of the men below me turned glossy. Everything was pink, fire coming from both sides of my head. And there was a sound — it was like the sound of the planes hitting the building on 9/11, a weird, guttural, discordant sound. Not like an explosion. And then afterwards I heard the sound when they played one of the films, the videotape [of the World Trade Center on 9/11, on television] and it was like a shock: That is the sound of the lightning — the plane going into the building.

"This is a very intense time in my life. The first part of my life was a leading up to this, a preparation. You learn a lot. You shouldn't hold on to things, to neuroses. People — artists — think they have to hold on to their neuroses, their pains, or they won't be a good actor anymore or a good artist. That's the Liar. The Liar tells you that. You hold on to them, you'll just wind up a lonely person. People become lonely with time, and the fame has moved on to someone else. You have to heal, you have to maintain relationships and get rid of dysfunction and neurosis. That's why we say the Our Father: 'Deliver us from evil.'

"I get letters from people — 'You swore in this movie,' or whatever. I reply, 'Yes, I play sinners.' "

I asked him at the end how long he had spoken to John Paul. He paused and said he didn't know. "I can't really remember. It wasn't longer than five minutes with me and ten minutes with my family. When I left, I was happy. I just felt happiness. We all left together."

Jim Caviezel gave me a beautiful rendering of a moment and, in a way, of his life. One senses he will go on to great work, for he is that best kind of artist, one who knows he is another worker in the vineyard who has much to do, and none of it without meaning.

CHAPTER NINE

Belief

By the end of his reign, John Paul was probably the most famous man in the world — the leader of more than a billion Catholics, a man who was seen by more human beings with their actual eyes than any leader in history. And he was not only famous but loved.

One reason: From the time he became pope he attempted to evangelize to everyone, wherever they were, in far-flung countries, on distant continents. He is famously the most traveled pope in history, and he made his journeys as if eager to show that everyone on earth — every one of us — is equally deserving of love, attention, respect. He made a strategic decision early in his papacy to focus attention on the young, on those who had not been fully informed of or taught the faith. He loved them and saw them as the future of the world. They loved him back: There were countless young people who filled the streets of Rome during his funeral crying, "Santo Subito."

★ ★ ★

Every time he arrived in a new country, John Paul would not travel upon its ground until he had first kissed its soil. He would get off the plane, walk down the stairs, kneel, bend, and kiss the ground, the earth. He did this in Istanbul, Managua, Dublin; in Lebanon, Sarajevo, Mexico City; in Zimbabwe and the Ivory Coast.

Who could forget it after having seen it? Who would not be moved? We could sense that by kissing the earth he was kissing Creation, the God-rich, God-inhabited, God-made place around us. By kissing the earth he was also kissing a singular and specific place, a patch of ground inhabited by a particular people with a particular culture, history, and tradition.

"There is a funny thing about the pope as communicator," a young priest and professor, Father John Wauck, told me in Rome over lunch in 2003. "John Paul doesn't believe in words as much as deeds. He is a believer in action — in what is *done* — far more than what is said and written." Father John is a young intellectual, and I'd expected him to talk to me about the pope's encyclicals, but he was more engaged by a passing reference I'd made to the pope's travels. I said it seemed to me an attempt to show that everyone on earth is deserving of love. I'd said I found it moving that in spite of his infirmity he continued to kiss the ground.

"Yes!" said Father John. "He travels to those countries and hugs the child, he meets with Agca, he goes to his prison cell and forgives him. The power of this kind of action is that it provokes human *thought.* The action is seen by human beings who see it and think: *What do I think of that?* And their private and personal answer to that question tells them a lot."

This struck me because I think it touches on or speaks to the often unarticulated reaction people had when the pope visited: *He makes you think of what you think. Some celebrated people leave you daydreaming, but John Paul left people uncovering their real and actual thoughts about life.*

Father John was just warming up. "John Paul comes to your country, and instead of going to dinner with your strongman or president, he kisses the ugly black tarmac. And then he goes to a school where poor children are educated, and he listens to their chorus, and he smiles. He communicates what's important through action, not words. This is an intuitive gift in a twentieth-century leader."

But here is a paradox:

This pope was famous and beloved, but many of those who loved him by instinct did not necessarily possess a sure sense of what he thought. It was strange: He was beloved for what he stood for, and yet a lot of people didn't know exactly what he stood for.

He is admired in many quarters because he would not back down in the face of various establishments' criticism and disagreement, in the face of their implicit promise that they would love him if only he would change his mind about things. As a friend once said, "This pope is the only leader in the world who doesn't care what the *New York Times* thinks of him."

We love him for not having backed down. But if you asked someone weeping in the crowd as he passed, "Not backing down from what?" chances are they may not have a very exact sense of the answer.

Even biographies of John Paul tended not to dwell on what he believed. Most of them tell you the stories of his life, in chronology, with dates of important encyclicals and the correct spelling in English of small, hard-to-pronounce Polish towns in which he lived. They tell you with precision how long he was in what hospital for what illness, and what he said when he spoke to the United Nations. They locate John Paul within history and explain his standing as a political and cultural figure.

But they often seem to avoid speaking at any great length of what he believed at his core, which is odd because what he believed is the reason for his greatness, the explanation of his power. It is the thing that puts him in history in the first place.

So I am going to attempt to speak a little of what he believed, based on what he told us in his writings, speeches, and comments. The subject is too big and too full of philosophical complexity to be fully mined in one book, or to be mined by me. John Paul wrote millions of words, and he was writing right up to the end.

But as I came to understand him, I came to more fully understand my own belief. By reading him, I felt I came to more fully know me, and to more fully *know* what I knew.

As to the obvious: Father Richard John Neuhaus said to me in an interview in

2003, succinctly and with a bit of a smile, "The pope believes what the Catholic Church believes. And the Catholic Church believes what the pope believes."

The pope believes in the Creation (God made and makes the world), the Incarnation (God bodily enters human history as Jesus Christ), the Resurrection (Christ, crucified, rises to be with the Father, who is also God, in heaven), and the Redemption (Christ's death and life have won and win you everlasting life, if you choose that life, and him).

But individual Christians bring their own emphases, complexities, and insights to these beliefs. So do popes.

John Paul as an intellectual, a creative and artistic human being, had particular gradations of thought, or rather, ways of looking at the fundamentals and approaching them that were distinctive to him. They reflected his cast of mind, temperament, experiences, and personality.

"He's a humanist through and through," said Father Neuhaus, "and he's a Christian humanist. If you look at his writings . . . he has two key phrases, number one, 'Man is the only creature that God has made for Himself,' and then the other, and perhaps the more important, that the revelation of

Jesus Christ is not only the revelation of God to man but of man to himself. The Christian Gospel is the revelation of man to himself . . ."

Neuhaus continued, "To live in the splendor of truth — [this is] his theme. If you want to find one Bible text that encapsulates him, Saint Paul was writing to the Corinthians — First Corinthians. You recall that in the first twelve chapters of First Corinthians he is discussing all these problems — factions and controversies and disagreements. . . . And then at the end of chapter twelve, Saint Paul says, 'Let me show you a more excellent way.' And then of course comes verse thirteen, the great love. And that phrase, 'Let me show you a more excellent way,' is what the entire life and ministry and persona of John Paul II is about."

After I talked to Neuhaus, I went to a Bible to read all of verse thirteen of Corinthians. It's the one we've all heard read aloud at weddings. "If I speak with the tongues of men and of angels, but have not love, I am become sounding brass, or a clanging cymbal. . . . Love suffereth long and is kind; love envieth not; love vaunteth not itself, is not puffed up. . . . [Love] rejoiceth with the truth. . . ."

★ ★ ★

Where others teach that man does not find himself until he finds God, John Paul gives an emphatic yes and then adds this: Man does not become his truest and most real self unless and until he also finds man.

John Paul believed that man is by nature part of a whole, that he does not exist alone. He lives in a society with other men, who are, like him, God's children. And it is in giving to man, in giving until it hurts, that man in the deepest way finds God. *For God himself is a constant giving.*

The pope believed that all of us, all of the human beings alive in the world right now, are a community of individuals who travel through history together. And we travel with similar luggage.

Each of us struggles through primary and essential questions that we cannot avoid once we reach or approach maturity. Why was I born? What is the meaning of life, and its purpose? Where and how can I find happiness? Why is life so full of pain and difficulty? How should we live, by what model or principles or arrangements?

A great mystery embraces our lives, John Paul said. Then he added something that has been to me deeply inspiring:

201

These questions we ask do not come only from your restless mind, and are not just products of your very human anxiety. *They come from God.* They are the beginning of the process by which you find him. God prompts them. He made you to ask.

The questions are, in fact, a kind of preparation for God, a necessary preamble to the story he wants to write on your heart. And the moment you ask them, your freedom has been set in motion. You become more sharply aware that there are choices.

This, in a way, is the beginning of morality, because there is no morality without freedom. Only in freedom can you turn toward what is good.

I am paraphrasing John Paul.

In fact, I am paraphrasing the encyclical that is often called his masterpiece, "Veritatis Splendor," "The Splendor of Truth."

You probably cannot have the understanding that John Paul speaks of with regard to struggling through to the truth without having had to struggle through to it yourself. John Paul, throughout his life, had big things to wrestle with. And that is part of how he knew others did too.

The struggle he speaks of is a struggle he knew firsthand, and it is a struggle that he felt *emotionally.*

Consider here his childhood, which in all of us is a first and unforgettable presentation of life.

Karol Wojtyla, as I've written, was born in the spring of 1920, the third child and second son of Emilia and Karol. A baby sister had died a few years earlier. Young Karol seems to have been born by temperament to be happy. He was a thoughtful and placid Polish boy who loved sports, soccer, ice skating, and hockey, who loved to walk and climb, and who in time felt a pull toward the arts. He was pudgy as a child, round faced, rather tall, intellectually quick.

So that is how he was born, going forward with happiness.

But the life he was born into became little by little overlaid with misfortune. His mother's health was always delicate; she died when he was eight years old. He found out when he came home one day from grade school. A neighborhood woman came out and hugged him and told him his mother was in heaven. He was surprised, then accepting, but it was years before he spoke about her, and when he

wrote a poem about her ten years later —
"O Mother, my extinct beloved" — it
spoke of a loss that would not be comforted.

It was only his first. His older brother,
Edmund, his only living sibling, had at the
time of his mother's death been away at
medical school in Kraków. Edmund was a
neighborhood star — popular, humorous,
and busy — and Karol revered him. When
Edmund was home, there was joy in the
air. Edmund received his medical degree in
1930, at the age of twenty-four, and became an intern, working in a city hospital
in a small town near Wadowice, where the
Wojtylas lived.

But two years after graduation Edmund
died suddenly, shockingly, of scarlet fever,
which he'd caught in the wards during an
epidemic. He had been working around
the clock and was worn down.

This was another terrible blow, one John
Paul II would later suggest was worse than
the loss of his mother, both because of its
tragic aspects — Edmund, with everything
ahead of him — and because Karol
Wojtyla was now old enough, at twelve, to
fully absorb the idea of death.

Now he would be brought up by a father
in mourning. Old Karol was a responsible

and even-tempered man who was conscientious in caring for his son and seeing to his spiritual education. But they were lonely together. They pushed their beds together in their apartment and slept in the same room. What had been a peaceful house was now a quiet one.

And old Karol was a limited man, or perhaps it is fairer to say he was not multifaceted like his son. He was a retired soldier, but mostly he had been a clerk and was now on a pension. He was an ardent Catholic and a sober one. After his wife's death he had taken young Karol to a series of Marian shrines, as if to tell him: This now is your mother.

Young Karol was not limited. He was expansive, not tidy and restricted. He wanted to be a poet — no, an actor — no, a philosopher! He had the broader personal vision of an artist — he could go on to do anything, everything was open, even if he was an obscure child living with a sad man in a small apartment. Karol could be a great man of literature, or a great man of the stage. Even better, a great man of his people.

Karol grew, finished high school. He was eighteen years old when World War II began raging. Poland was occupied by the Nazis, and young Karol became a factory worker. He came home from his shift one afternoon with a friend and entered his flat. It was 1941; young Karol was twenty.

His father was in bed, but in an odd and ungainly position. He seemed to be resting, but it was as if he'd gotten half out of bed and then stayed there. Young Karol went to lift him and felt his cold hands. He began to cry, sitting there on the bed, holding his father's lifeless body.

He had not been there when his mother died, he had not been there when his brother died, now he had not been there when his father died.

And now there was no one else in the family. There was no one else to lose.

Here is the scene as painted by the Polish journalist Gian Franco Svidercoschi, in *Stories of Karol.* All through the night Karol kept watch over his father's body, saying to his friends, "I'm all alone. . . . At twenty I've already lost all the people I've loved!" He was despairing.

Svidercoschi writes, "There was something far deeper, something like an uprooting from everything that his father represented, via origins, tradition, family history and authority. It was like being violently ripped out of the soil in which he, the son, had grown until then." Karol began to talk "in an excited, frenetic manner" of the future, of plans that had to be confronted. "Karol's life could no longer be what it used to be. From that moment on, other questions, other inner torments, began to arise."

So this was his dark night of the soul. And in his loneliness and aloneness, he must have asked, "Why? What does this mean? What is the meaning? Am I alone?"

He came to believe more deeply than ever that he was not alone. He *chose*. He chose to follow his faith and dig deeper in it. He now began a journey to a deeper communion with God. But it didn't come without tears, and it didn't come without what seems to have been a certain existential horror.

Which seems to have hit him like a hammer, and which subtly informs "The Splendor of Truth."

We wonder, John Paul says, if there is a God. And while we think about this, we are all of us constantly drawn to "gods," to gods of our own making. We start to obey them and their demands — the god of pleasure or wealth, the god of ambition or excitement, the god of physical beauty or popularity.

But these gods are false. We've invented them. Or we begin to notice them and consciously or unconsciously honor them when our neighbor invents them. (Perhaps when the man next door parks his new speedboat in his driveway, you can't help but start to worship the god of prosperity who brings beautiful things you can park in front of your house. The wonderful thing about this god is that the fruits of worship are so quantifiable, in wealth in the bank say, or a new Lexus.)

False gods are alluring; but while we're looking at them or up to them, we are looking away from the real God. And when we look away from him, we become less able to see the truth. Which only gets us deeper into confusion. When you follow the god of the day, you wind up lost, on a path to nowhere.

But, the pope writes, do not be afraid. Even when we are following illusion, the true God hasn't died in us. The light of God is still within us, waiting.

If there is a phrase people think of when they think of John Paul, it is "Be not afraid." By the time the pope was a man, in his full maturity, he knew and was convinced that ultimately there was nothing to fear. "Be not afraid!" was his first announcement to the people of Rome and of the world when he became pope, and "Be not afraid" were the first words he said on his first trip to the United States, and in every trip to America thereafter. I think he said it most beautifully during the big open Mass in New York's Central Park on his last trip to America, on a Saturday, October 7, 1995.

There he said, in his final blessing to the people of New York, "Do not be afraid! I can see that Americans are not afraid. They are not afraid of the sun, they are not afraid of the wind, they are not afraid of 'today.' They are, generally speaking, brave, good people. And so I say to you today, always be brave. Do not be afraid. Do not be afraid. God is with you. Do not be afraid to search for God — then you will truly be the land of the free, the home of the brave. God bless America."

He spent so much time counseling against fear that you have to wonder what kind of fear he himself felt as he made his way through life, as he struggled through his aloneness and came to grips with what he believed, and as he came to understand the price he would pay to become what he was to become.

From his high school days his friends had asked him if he meant to be a priest, but he knew he would not. That wasn't the life he wanted, and he was certain in any case that he was not worthy of it. But as he studied philosophy, his faith continued to deepen. He followed the implications of this deepening, and began to consider going into seminary. As he considered the implications of that, he had to come face-to-face with a stark and immediate one: The Nazis were at that time closing the seminaries, literally nailing them shut. They didn't want more priests. Priests were a problem. If you were found studying for the priesthood, you'd pay a price: deportation to a work camp or death.

But there was more, and it was within him. In the series of interviews that became the 2000 bestseller *Crossing the Threshold of Hope*, the journalist Vittorio Messori asked John Paul about his exhortations to fearlessness. The pope replied, *"Of what should we not be afraid?* We should not fear *the truth about ourselves."* He spoke of how Saint Peter himself, the rock on which Christ had built his church, had told Christ to leave him, "for I am a sinful man." Peter *was* a sinful man. We all are, including popes. We are imperfect and "our hearts are anxious." But we cannot and should not let the fact of our unworthiness and flaws and failures build a wall between ourselves and God. We can't hide behind that wall with a kind of inverted pride that says, Oh, I'm so unworthy, and I'd know how unworthy I am better than you would.

"Christ knows our anguish best of all," the pope says. He knows better than anyone else what is inside us. And when the pope tells us to have no fear, when he cheers us with the knowledge that we do not have to be afraid, he is saying too, "Do not be afraid of God." Do not be afraid of God, John Paul said, but instead "invoke him." Call him Father. "God is with us. God, infinitely perfect, is not only with man, but He Himself became a man in Jesus Christ. *Do not be afraid of God who became a man!*"

Those are all John Paul's italics.

John Paul held that a major obstacle to belief in the modern world is a misunderstanding of what freedom actually *is.* The modern assumption is that freedom is absolute personal autonomy, the right to do what one wants. The great philosophers the pope studied as a young man working for his earned doctorates had strong things to say here. Hegel, whom Karol Wojtyla studied with interest, wrote persuasively of a master-slave paradigm between God and man. To bow to God makes man seem servile, obsequious, fearful, unfree. Marx, of course, argued that religious faith alienates people from their humanity, depriving them of their true nature. Ludwig Feuerbach, whom Wojtyla studied and pondered, taught in the nineteenth century that in place of love of God it was time that man acknowledged love of man as the true religion.

Much of modern secularism proceeded from the work of these philosophers. John Paul studied that work, absorbed it, and was not satisfied with it. He did not believe these thinkers had found the truth. As cardinal and pope he contradicted them but not with appeals to faith so much as with appeals to reason.

The pope argued that the master-slave paradigm did not stand up to the light of reason in part because it is obvious even to philosophy, even to philosophers, that God, even in the abstract, is good. It follows then that God created us as an expression of and a *part* of that goodness. He wanted to love us and befriend us. He could not therefore have created us to be his slaves. You want those you love to be free men and women who choose to love you of their own will.

John Paul argued in "Veritatis Splendor" that human freedom in fact finds its authenticity and fulfillment in acceptance of the law of God — a law that does not reduce or do away with human freedom but rather *protects and promotes* it. Human freedom and God's law are not in opposition.

The pope asserted that although you are free to choose this path or another, true freedom — real freedom, the freedom God gave you — is the freedom to know him, and follow him. John Paul quoted Saint Augustine: "To the extent to which we serve God we are free, while to the extent that we follow . . . sin, we are still slaves."

Those who follow the world and worship the antic gods man invents and elevates experience God's law as a burden, as a denial or restriction of freedom. But those who will be satisfied with nothing but the truth are driven forward to find God's essence.

Freedom was one of John Paul's longtime intellectual preoccupations. There can be no morality without it, he asserted, but it is not license to do evil. Deep in a man's conscience, John Paul said, he detects a law that he does not impose on himself but that holds him to obedience. It summons him to love good and avoid evil. And it can, when necessary, speak to his heart very specifically: "Do this; shun that."

This is the human conscience, which he defined as "the sanctuary of man, where he is alone with God, whose voice echoes within him." It is an interior dialogue of man with himself, but it is also a dialogue of man with God. Saint Bonaventure said conscience is like a herald or messenger of God: It does not and cannot command things on its own, but commands them as coming from God's authority, as a herald does when he proclaims the edict of the king. But moral conscience doesn't close man within an insurmountable and impenetrable solitude. It opens him to God. Conscience is the place where God speaks to man. And it has rights because it has duties.

The pope teaches that the power to decide what is good and what is evil does not belong to us, that the individual conscience is not a supreme tribunal. People say, "I must follow my conscience," but they must not do so under the illusion that a moral judgment is true merely because it has its origin in the conscience. When people accept that illusion, they will find that the claims of truth disappear, and in its place come other things, such as the idea that being at peace with oneself is enough. It isn't.

The pope reminds us that we must not lose sight of the idea that there is a real and universal truth about the good that is knowable by human reason. If we lose this, then the notion of conscience also changes. Conscience then is no longer an act of a person's intelligence in which is applied the knowledge of the good in a specific situation. The individual conscience does not have the prerogative of independently determining what is good and what is evil. If you take that path, you wind up with the mantra of individualism: Each of us is faced with his own truth, different from the truth of others; everything is relative. In this way, says John Paul, we wind up back with Pilate: "What is truth?"

God has already told us, and will continue to tell us, what is good and what is true.

★ ★ ★

All belief, all decisions to believe, take place within a context. Some ages tend to encourage faith and belief; some do not. John Paul long shared his concern about modern culture, specifically the culture of the West. He knew, as most of us do, that significant portions of that culture are disturbed — unduly violent, highly sexualized, destructive. We see this reflected in our media, on the news and in movies, in music and on television. We entertain ourselves with our disturbance.

John Paul's reservations about modern culture included the observation that it tends to separate man, to atomize us, to break us down into small parts of small spheres instead of lifting us as vibrant elements of a larger whole.

We are distracted by this atomizing culture. We are surrounded and saturated by images made by others and imposed, in a sense, on our consciousness. They don't usually have much to do with the real drama of man, which is the movement of his soul and spirit.

We are at home alone with Tivo and a glass of merlot; we are home alone Web surfing; we are out on the teeming streets alone with our iPods, listening to self-selected symphonies.

John Paul saw this fragmentation. But he did not believe our culture forms an impassible barrier to belief. We are saved and united by the fact that we are who we are: humans. And a great fact of human life, he said, powerfully counters the atomization around us: the universal and unifying experience of thirsting for truth. We are oriented by nature, as human persons, to look for what is true.

This is something we all, gifted and slow, rich and poor, share.

In a way, he says, we are all like Adam. We are not, as men and women on earth, only part of life on earth, like a dog or a flower. John Paul believed, as Cardinal Avery Dulles has written, that we are special, that "the human person, created in the image and likeness of God and called to share eternally in the inner life of the triune God, stands above all visible creation." As a result, John Paul teaches, we yearn, we quest. You can see this in man's constant search for advances in art and science and literature and quantum physics, in all the areas in which we seek to break through and discover.

We're always reaching, even when we don't know what we are trying to grasp. We have a natural desire — we were born with it — to find what is true, and real. And we have a tendency, each of us, not to rest until we have found it.

So that is where John Paul starts when he thinks of modern man, and this is what he knows: The truth exists and can be seen. "It shines forth in the work of the Creator and, in a special way, in man." And more. There are absolutes, moral absolutes, and they are real and alive and pertinent to all the ages and eras of man.

Here we get to the central core of John Paul. We know his most famous words were, "Be not afraid." But here are the words that come from his very first encyclical as pope, which he wrote himself, with time to ponder what his message would be. He wrote knowing that this encyclical might turn out to be his only one, his only major message to the world. The pope he succeeded had served for only thirty-three days. John Paul was aware that powerful forces were arrayed against him from the communist world. His first encyclical could be his last. So he had every reason to want it to include the most important and crucial thing he had to say.

These are, literally, the first words of

that document: "The Redeemer of man, Jesus Christ, is the center of the universe and of history." *The center of the universe and of history.* No mistaking those words, that message. Four sentences later he speaks of "the key truth of faith which Saint John expressed at the beginning of his Gospel: 'The Word became flesh and dwelt among us,' and elsewhere: 'God so loved the world that he gave his only Son, that whoever believes in him should not perish but have eternal life.' "

All of John Paul's subsequent encyclicals might be considered elaborations or expansions on the first. Later, in his tenth encyclical, he would say, "The answer to every one of man's fundamental questions is given by Jesus Christ. Or rather *is* Jesus Christ, himself."

So from the beginning John Paul was telling us that Christ himself is at the very center of our reality and his papacy.

But who is Christ? "Veritatis Splendor" again. We know exactly who Christ is because he gave us a "self portrait" in the Sermon on the Mount, his very first sermon. Christ reveals himself in the Beatitudes that frame that sermon. These two compose the Magna Carta of Gospel teaching on *how to live.* The Beatitudes promise the good that opens man up to eternal life; we learn from them, in fact, "the attitudes and understanding of the moral life."

In the Sermon on the Mount, Christ says, "Blessed are the poor, for theirs is the kingdom of God. Blessed are the hungry, for they shall be filled. . . . Blessed shall you be when men shall hate you, and when they shall separate you, and shall reproach you, for the Son of Man's sake. Be glad on that day, for your rewards will be great in heaven. . . . Love your enemies, do good to them that hate you. . . . Pray for those who curse you. . . . Do unto others as you would that men would do to you. . . . Love your enemies, do good and help them. . . . Be merciful. . . . Judge not, condemn not. Forgive."

This, says John Paul, is Christ's "self-portrait." And it is, he says, something else: It is an "invitation" to join him.

What else do we know of Christ? John Paul asks. That he is one of the Holy Trinity that comprises God; that he is part of the triune God; that he is both God and Man; that he was sent to earth to live among us and to suffer by our hands, through which suffering he would save us.

It is Christ, the pope teaches, "who fully

discloses man to himself." Christ is the teacher, he is "patient and sensitive," he is not just a figure of the past, a person who lived at some point in history. He is ever present in the world. He is here, *now.* And if you want to understand yourself thoroughly you must draw near to him. For when a man enters into Christ he not only comes to know and love God, he comes to have "a deeper wonder at himself."

Christ, says John Paul, knows all about mankind's efforts to discover the meaning of life. No one knows humanity as he does: He is its great expert.

Christ's way of acting, his words and deeds, constitute, says John Paul, a perfect expression of the moral life.

Do you want to heal your fractured, fragmented world? Do you want to heal your fractured, fragmented self? Then follow him, for he is the great healer of man who gives us the answer to the question: How should I live?

Jesus, John Paul teaches, asks us to follow him and imitate him. Being a follower of Christ means giving all. It becomes a desire to live in and for perfect love. But this isn't an invitation restricted to a small group of people. It is an invitation open to every human on the planet. And it *is* possible for every human on the planet. How? "With God, all things are possible." How can we give ourselves completely? How could it be possible to give all? It is possible only because he dwells within you, the pope answers. You could never imitate Christ or live out the love of Christ on your own strength alone. You become capable of this love only by virtue of a gift received. It is a gift from Christ, and it is a gift of the Holy Spirit, whose first fruit is charity — the wish to be charitable, followed by charitable action.

You start to love. That love isn't learned; it is given, by God. You cannot acquire it through your own abilities, says John Paul, because it is beyond your abilities. You get it from God, who transforms the human heart.

The pope believed that God gave us all, long ago, the essential rules of the road: the Ten Commandments, the indispensable beginning point for how to live. In the commandments, the pope said, God tells us what we have to know. They begin with God telling us that he is God. He makes himself known as the One who alone is good, who is faithful in his love of man, and who asks us, despite our flaws, to be holy.

Why did God give man his law? To restore man's peaceful harmony with the Creator himself, and with all of creation, said John Paul. The Commandments are a gift to man — a restorer of harmony — and they function as both a promise and a sign. Christ told us to keep them, for they lead to life. We know this from Christ's own lips when, in the New Testament, he was questioned by a wealthy young man who wanted salvation. "If you wish to enter into life, keep the commandments," Christ said.

The central commandment? Christ spoke of it, said John Paul: the commandment to love thy neighbor. In this commandment, says the pope, we find an expression of the singular dignity of the human person.

The "negative" precepts of the commandments are enumerated by the famous shalt nots: Thou shalt not murder, commit adultery, steal; thou shalt not bear false witness. These are clear prohibitions. They tell us of the need, the necessity, to protect human life, and the communion of marriage, and private property, and truthfulness, and reputations. These "negative" commandments are the basic conditions for loving your neighbor, and they are a basic proof of that love.

But they are only the first steps, the starting point on your journey to freedom. For as Saint Augustine said, "The beginning of freedom is to be free from crimes. . . ." Once you are without crimes, you begin to lift your head higher, and aspire. So, Jesus Christ said, love your God and love your neighbor. These two commandments — not negatives, not shalt nots, but positive commandments about how to live most happily — are, according to the pope, profoundly connected.

When Christ was asked, "Who is your neighbor?" he replied with the famous story of the Good Samaritan. For no clear motive of self-benefit, a good man helped a beaten man. The good man took on himself the responsibility of comforting and caring for the wounded man. Without love of neighbor, says John Paul, genuine love for God is not possible. He quotes Saint John the Apostle: "If anyone says, 'I love God,' and hates his brother, he is a liar; for he who does not love his brother whom he has seen, cannot love God whom he has not seen."

The commandments are not a minimum

limit of what must not be done; they are a path involving a moral and spiritual journey toward perfection. And, again, toward love.

Respecting the moral demands of the commandments represents the essential ground in which the desire for perfection can take root. But perfection itself requires more. The commandments, John Paul noted, can tell us what to do, but they cannot do it for us.

After respecting and obeying comes the giving of the self. And this involves — again — freedom. Or as John Paul puts it, "the particular dynamic of freedom's growth toward maturity."

What can teach us, beyond the commandments and the words of Christ? The apostles were great instructors, says John Paul: They, too, told us how to live. You can see this in their letters, which contain the interpretation, made under the guidance of the Holy Spirit, of Christ's precepts. From the beginning the apostles were vigilant as to the conduct of Christians, just as they were vigilant for the handing down of the sacraments. The first Christians, coming both from the Jewish people and from the Gentiles, differed from the pagans not only in their faith and their liturgy but also in the witness of their moral conduct.

And there is the church, said John Paul, to which Christ entrusted the promotion and preservation of the faith. The tradition that comes from the apostles progresses in the church to this day, under the assistance of the Holy Spirit. It is the Holy Spirit that guarantees that Christ's teachings will be preserved, expounded, and applied. The church, prompted by the Holy Spirit, tells the truth of Christ. But, John Paul teaches, the church has not ceased to contemplate the mystery of God made flesh. The church reflects continually on it, and is and must be eager to reconcile divine revelation with the demands of human reason.

It is important to remember, John Paul teaches, that God himself loves and cares, in the most literal and basic sense, for all creation. But he provides for man differently from the way in which he provides for others in his handiwork. He cares for man not "from without," through the laws of physical nature, but "from within," through reason, which, by its natural knowledge of God's eternal law, is able to show man the right direction to take in his free actions.

God, the pope says, created man to be

above the rest of creation. And so God calls man to participate in his own providence, since he desires to guide the world — the world of nature and the world of human persons — through man himself.

What if, with all this good direction — the Ten Commandments, the words of Christ, the leadership of the apostles — you choose to do wrong? That is sin, which the church defines as a separation from God. Mortal sin separates man from God, removes him from God's grace; it is a turning away. And some immoral choices are seriously evil. The Second Vatican Council gives a number of examples of such wrong acts: "Whatever is hostile to life itself, such as any kind of homicide, genocide, abortion, euthanasia and voluntary suicide; whatever violates the integrity of the human person, such as mutilation, physical and mental torture and attempts to coerce the spirit; whatever is offensive to human dignity, such as subhuman living conditions, arbitrary imprisonment, deportation, slavery, prostitution and trafficking in women and children; degrading conditions of work which treat laborers as mere instruments of profit, and not as free responsible persons: all these and the like are a disgrace, and so long as they infect human civilization they contaminate those who inflict them more than those who suffer injustice, and they are a negation of the honor due to the Creator."

John Paul teaches that human acts are moral acts because they express the goodness or evil of the individual who performs them. They do not produce a change merely in the state of affairs outside of man, they give moral definition to the very person who performs them. The pope quotes Saint Gregory of Nyssa: "All things subject to change and to becoming never remain constant, but continually pass from one state to another, for better or worse. . . . [H]uman life is always subject to change . . . but here birth does not come about by a foreign intervention . . . it is the result of free choice."

We are in a certain way our own parents, creating ourselves as we will, by our decisions.

So if you are living well and morally, don't become conceited: *You are also your next act.* If you are living badly and sinfully, don't become demoralized: *You can become a saint.*

What all of this means in the end is that

God is with you as you search for him, with you as you find him, with you as you try to understand and do the right. It means you are *not* alone.

And if you are not alone, well, you have little to fear. Again, "Be not afraid."

Why would you be afraid? You are not only not alone, you walk with the most powerful figure in Creation. And with him all things are possible. Literally, all things are possible with God. This is not a pious saying; it is the truth.

So, these are some of John Paul's beliefs, in brief, and drawn with some obviousness and crudeness. He did not draw them so. And he held them truly, passionately.

And yet this very human pope had his own difficulties, and knowing of them is inspiring.

John Paul had what seemed to me an extraordinary interest in something that might be surprising in a pope, or perhaps surprising if you forget that the pope was a man. It can perhaps be referred to as the struggle of the Ardent Christian Who Seems to Lose Christ. The struggle of one who has already found God, made his decision for God, and adheres to God but who has, at the same time and sometimes for a long time, lost the consolation that that knowledge brings, or lost even the interior knowledge that God exists.

Imagine that trial. Imagine that you have given your life to God, your whole life to his service, as a minister or in the convent or as a monk in a monastery. Imagine it as a mother who has built her entire family around faith, and then seems to lose her love and certitude. Imagine beginning to lose the *feeling* of the knowledge that the life you gave was given to — something real. You have doubts. You wonder if you were deluded. Maybe you made a mistake. Maybe to some degree, therefore, your whole life was a mistake.

This phenomenon has been given a famous phrase, "the dark night of the soul." It is sung of in the canticles of Saint John of the Cross. Interestingly, John Paul had always been drawn to Saint John, and he wrote his doctoral thesis on John's thought. The "dark night" was experienced too by Saint Teresa of Avila, to whom the pope was drawn. Saint Thérèse of Lisieux, a hero of the twentieth-century church and a doctor of the church, also spoke of it.

And now we know, and the pope would have known long ago, for he was her friend and her great supporter (he sped her toward the process of canonization; she was beatified only seven years after her death) that Mother Teresa of Calcutta — Mother Teresa! — also knew the dark night.

In the May 2003 issue of *First Things*, the scholarly American magazine of religious belief, there is a quote from "The Soul of Mother Teresa: Hidden Aspects of Her Interior Life," by the Reverend Brian Kolodiejchuk, who is the postulator in the Vatican for Mother Teresa's cause for sainthood. He has conducted a lengthy and comprehensive investigation of her communications throughout her life with her spiritual directors. He found that she had experienced four stages of her spiritual life, and the one that lasted longest, as long as the previous and happier three, was her own dark night. Father Kolodiejchuk writes, "Throughout 1946 and 1947, Mother Teresa experienced a profound union with Christ. But soon after she left the convent and began her work among the destitute and dying on the street, the visions and locutions ceased, and she experienced a spiritual darkness that would remain with her until her death. It is hard to know what is more to be marveled at: that this twentieth-century commander of a worldwide apostolate and army of charity should have been a visionary contemplative at heart; or that she should have persisted in radiating invincible faith and love while suffering inwardly from the loss of spiritual consolation. In letters written during the 1950s and 1960s to Fr. Van Exem, Archbishop Périer, and to later spiritual directors, Fr. L. T. Picachy, S.J., and Fr. J. Neuner, S.J., she disclosed feelings of doubt, loneliness, and abandonment. God seemed absent, heaven empty, and bitterest of all, her own suffering seemed to count for nothing, '. . . just that terrible pain of loss, of God not wanting me, of God not being God, of God not really existing.' "

Of God not really existing. This from a woman who had built her life around him.

First Things wondered about, and offered an answer to, the meaning of Mother Teresa's private writings. "It means that the missionary foundress who called herself 'God's pencil' was not the God-intoxicated saint many of us had assumed her to be. We may prefer to think that she spent her days in a state of ecstatic mystical union with God, because that would get us ordinary worldlings off the hook. How else could this unremarkable woman, no different from the rest of us, bear to throw her lot in with the poorest of the poor, sharing their meager diet and rough clothing, wiping leprous sores and enduring the agonies of the dying, for so many years without respite, unless she were somehow lifted above it all, shielded by spiritual endorphins? Yet we have her own testimony that what made her self-negating work possible was not a subjective experience of ecstasy but an objective relationship to God shorn of the sensible awareness of God's presence."

To live as she lived without the consolations of belief, to do what she did without the reliable feeling of internal joy or even security — that is heroic.

It is interesting that John Paul was drawn to that kind of hero, inspiring that he had such deep respect for her questing, doubting, honest mind. And that knowing what he knew, he pushed and even rushed forward her cause for sainthood.

CHAPTER TEN

Some Different Kinda Pope!

In September of 1979, when I was a writer at CBS News, John Paul was a new pope, and people in the New York broadcast center were still getting used to him. One afternoon the bells on the AP wire machine — it was the old kind that buzzed and printed out thick rolls of paper, and rang when important news occurred — resounded through the room. The editor walked over and read the story. It was a report from Vatican City. It said the new pope had issued a long pastoral letter on the human body, on marriage and sex and love. The editor began reading and then looked up. "This is some different kinda pope!" he said.

What the wires were reporting was that the pope had begun giving a series of general audiences in which he addressed the subject of human sexuality. He spoke so lovingly about physical love that it was startling. The last time a pope had spoken at any great length on issues dealing with sexuality was fifteen years before, when Pope Paul VI restated the church's position on artificial birth control. The message was: It is not good, not right, and not sanctioned. The declaration proved to be explosive in so many ways in so many circles that barely anyone in the Vatican had mentioned sex since, and the church continued with its paradoxical reputation as an antisex institution that had historically encouraged the most sensual art and the most passionate thinking in all the world, not to mention its love for big families and fruitfulness.

John Paul had once been a parish priest and as parish priest he had been a marriage counselor. To some degree, all parish priests are. He counseled those who were married and experiencing difficulties in their relationships, and those who were about to be married. The counseling was key to the man John Paul would become. If he had been a church bureaucrat through much of his career and worked in administrative offices that specialized in finances or diplomacy, as some of his predecessor popes had done, he would not have had the experience he gained talking with people on intimate terms about how they really lived and what they really felt, struggled with, and questioned. He might not have had to ponder their lives and ponder church teaching as it affected those lives.

What he learned as priest and then bishop became part of the pope's definitive statement on, and response to, the modern sexual revolution that, even when he was a young man in his midthirties, was beginning to sweep the world.

What the priest Karol Wojtyla came to believe, he later said, was that the tradition of Catholic sexual teaching had become too much dominated by the idea of the soul trying to master the body, as if the body were a rather wicked thing waiting to trip one up on the road to salvation. This, he felt, reflected a false reading of church teaching, and was neglectful of certain truths that hadn't sufficiently been stated, at least recently. For one thing, the false reading seemed not to take into account what John Paul exalted as the quiet union of body and soul when we are at our best and fully alive and truly experiencing life in the broadest and most joy-filled way.

The pope made it clear in his papal conversations that he was concerned that there was too great a tendency in Western society to view the human body in a confused and superficial way. We view it as something that is outside us, something that belongs to us that we must control, as something that is on some level detached from us. But, he argued, you cannot separate the soul from the body. They are united. They do not exist in opposition to each other, they are together, and together they make you. You cannot separate what your body does from what your will does. Not only that, the particular body you have and were given was meant for the particular soul you were given.

So your body isn't a pretty wrapped box with a gift inside called a soul. The box and the gift are one and enmeshed, together.

And we know this, or sense it, in many ways, he said. When you are a new mother and hold your newborn in your arms in those first weeks and months when your body is close to your child and meshed with your child and feeding your child — that is a moment, John Paul says, that tells us something about the unity of body and soul. He paints a portrait of Rebecca, in the Old Testament, seeing Isaac coming across the field — she sees him and her heart leaps. She sees him and already she loves him. It's a beautiful image because it speaks of a wholeness: It isn't only her body that is engaged but her very essence, her spirit and soul. All of her. In the New Testament, John Paul notes, there is the passion of Jesus Christ — a profoundly physical and spiritual agony in which the physical and the spiritual are part of each other. This, too, suggests the facts of the wholeness and unity of the human person.

The pope was keen to make the point that there is always a tendency among Christians to think of the salvation of the soul and the mastering of the body as if the body were something to be denied or indulged. Carried to an extreme, this conception suggests the soul is the seat of all goodness, and the body is the seat of all badness. But that is not so. After all, as John Paul points out, the soul is the seat of pride, which is a sin; your arms and your stomach are not.

Well, he says, we must shake off this modern conception of the body, and see it in a different way.

The pope began his statements on the body by meditating on the story of Adam and Eve in the Garden of Eden. Adam was all alone, without anyone to speak to, with no use even for language. He had no one to touch or to look into the eyes of. He was lonely, and God could see it. But there were some parts of this loneliness that must have been intellectually fruitful. For one thing, Adam must have come to understand that he was alone in part because he wasn't an animal, or a tree. He was different. He came to know himself as a person, a human being. But he saw there was no one around him like him. He needed another human person. And so Adam was given Eve.

The former *Time* magazine correspondent Wilton Wynn, who converted to Catholicism after covering John Paul for more than ten years, later wrote that as a former Baptist he was struck by the pope's teaching. The pope often taught, said Wynn, quoting John Paul, that " 'the word Adam does not mean man, it means human. God created Adam, the human, and then divided it so there was male and female.' " This, said Wynn, meant that "instead of saying man was created and the woman was created from him, [John Paul] puts it on a level of perfect equality."

John Paul taught that Eve was different from Adam but part of him, and *together* they composed a fuller image of God. Adam recognizes Eve as "flesh of my flesh." In doing so, he becomes part of a complete giving and receiving of another human being, and this, says John Paul, is the great "moment of communion," when man in his duality becomes "the image of God."

So not until he was two was Adam fully one. Eve was the completer, the easer of loneliness. He had a body and she had a body, and together they were one.

None of this story is accident, the pope suggests, and none of it is without deep meaning for all human beings.

John Paul often noted that Christianity is the only religion that promises the resurrection of the body, not just the soul. Many Catholics forget this, even though every time we go to Mass we say the Apostles' Creed: "We look for the resurrection of the dead, and the life of the world to come." Such a doctrine leaves you wondering how. In exactly what way does that happen? Which body is resurrected — the innocent one when you were a toddler, the strong one you had when you were twenty-five, the old one you died with? We don't know and aren't told, but the central message stands: Catholicism isn't only about the salvation of our souls but the salvation of the body.

But there is more to learn from the story of Adam and Eve, John Paul says. Their giving to each other shows that sexuality was built into men and women from the beginning. And in the beginning it didn't involve any shame.

Shame, the pope says, is the result of "fear" — fear that we are or have become an *object*, fear that we actually see another person as an object, or use him or her as an object of pleasure or desire. George Weigel here offers understanding of the pope's thinking. "Sin, the pope explains, enters the world as a corruption of genuine self-giving, which is motivated by love. When that self-giving is experienced as restraint rather than fulfillment, love decays into lust, and the icon of created goodness . . . that was sexual love 'in the beginning,' in the pope's words, is broken." What happens then? Human beings "lose their 'original certainty' that the world is good and we are fit for living in it. . . ." Here, Weigel says, explaining the pope's thinking, "The difference between male and female, once a source of identity in communion, becomes a source of confrontation."

Mere lust shatters the communion between people. But the Christian sexual ethic, the pope asserts, redeems sexuality from that dead end. Weigel again: "Far from prohibiting *eros,* the Christian ethic liberates eros" for — in the pope's words now — "full and mature spontaneity" in which the "attraction" of the sexes finds its fulfillment in mutual self-giving. This, John Paul argues, is not the banishment or denial of desire, it is the full *expression* of desire.

The pope then went on to celebrate marital love, and I believe this was the part of John Paul's statements that made my editor at CBS say, "This is some different kinda pope!" Because when the pope spoke of sexuality within marriage, he expressed himself in a way that showed no awkwardness or reservation, but rather robust warmth. Sexual love in marriage, he says, is an act of worship, of deep human creativity. The "language of the body" provides a way of encountering the sacred — and the sacred is a way of encountering God. The sexual giving of oneself, he says, makes the world a better place; *it is, in fact, a way to sanctify the world.*

When I read this, I found it startling. Everyone thinks the church tries to diminish sex or make it less central or important. But this pope is saying it's bigger than you know, it's transcendent.

The pope teaches that it is in the unity of body and soul that the person is the subject of his own moral acts. You cannot dissociate the moral act from the bodily dimension of its exercise. The human person in his totality is a soul that expresses itself in a body, and a body informed by an immortal spirit. They stand and fall together.

These teachings carry through into obvious ones on sexuality outside of marriage. Michael Novak: "Adultery and so forth introduce a discordance that violates the unity of body and soul. It is a violation of one's nature, and it starts the chords ringing discordantly. It does so pleasantly and bewitchingly — that is why Dante put such sins in the less terrible rings of hell, because there seems to be a kind of sharing. But it appears to be full and permanent when it is not, it is only temporary." Sexual activity outside the sacrament of marriage "compromises the soul's honesty and integrity. It makes it *doubt* itself. It launches a principle of untruthfulness into the soul and the body, and that devalues both over time." It leads, he said, to "the jading of everyday life."

That is a wonderful phrase to sum up our time, "the jading of everyday life." A time when both men and women are more confused by one another, more defended against one another; when they speak more disparagingly about their relations and are more cynical about the other's motives, and their own. The pope suggests this unhappiness is not the result of the war between men and women, but rather of not understanding that men and women are not, in fact, and were not made to be, at war. They were made to complete one another, in trust, with authenticity and delight.

Why did the pope turn his attention to this subject? In part to more fully explain and expand upon the church's true teachings; in part to make new what had been forgotten or distorted; in part to give instruction to priests of the church, so they in turn could help their flock; in part because John Paul knew, even back in the seventies, that the meaning of human sexuality was a rising issue of fascination and anxiety in the modern world.

And in part, I suspect, because of this: We are suffering, in the West, through an imbalanced period of cultural history, a time that seems to mark both an obsessive interest in and an anxious, even combative attitude toward the human body.

We seem not so comfortable in our skin;

we war with our nature. Sex is treated as a search for the perfect moment with the perfect man or woman; there is more sexual information and instruction than ever before, but all of it seems predicated on dissatisfaction. In many of our schools we teach our sons and daughters that sexuality is a mechanical function freed from meaning. We teach them about condoms, their use and reliability. Then we feel discomfort when our children, as young adults, begin to treat sexuality as if were a function free of meaning and robbed of import. Women become angry with men — "You used me." And men with women — "You tricked me."

It is all so confused. And maybe the beginning of the confusion, its source, is an inability to see the unity of body and soul, and the deep significance, therefore, of the sexual act. In the West we are in such a paradoxical position: We obsess on sex in our schools and media as if it were the most important thing in the world, and yet our very obsession undercuts its importance, makes it banal, common, unimportant. We get it wrong. And if you get that wrong, nothing that follows is going to make much sense. "There is something about our bodies," Michael Novak mused to me, "that tells us what God is like. And if we mess that up we mess God up, too."

The pope's teachings on the body reflected, I think, his deep and natural comfort with the body, a comfort with the idea of our physical being. He lived a life in which he took great joy in his physicality; he was an athlete from boyhood on, playing soccer and hiking, kayaking, swimming. This was him being himself, using his body. I think of John Paul doing something he truly loved — hiking in the hills above Rome, and praying, and sometimes singing after praying. Up there in the mountains, in the air.

Such a life is worlds away from the funny modern relationship we have with our own bodies. We obsess on our physical form, making it slim, smooth, perfect. We tell ourselves we do this because we love our bodies and want them to be beautiful. But I wonder sometimes if we don't secretly fear our bodies. Thus we redesign them, are never satisfied with them, try against sense to insist they be young looking and perfect.

When I was questioning intellectuals and writers who study the pope on his teachings regarding the body and the soul, one man I spoke to was perplexed by my questions.

"You know the answers," he said. "It's all in that piece you wrote about Karen Hughes." This surprised me. I went back to the piece, which I'd published in the *Wall Street Journal*'s online editorial page on April 2002, after Bush adviser Hughes had announced she was going to leave the White House. Her departure struck me as a beautiful and heartening decision if, as I then assumed, it was driven by a desire to leave the grinding intensity of political work and return to the daily enjoyment of: life. So I wrote a piece called "Back to Life."

What is life? It is the nice big thing you enter each morning when the alarm goes off and you put your feet on the cool floor and then stand, with your hands on the bottom of your back, and look out the window.

Life is putting on coffee, picking up the newspaper and putting on the radio and listening for a few seconds to see if something huge and terrible happened last night. You can tell by the sound of the voices. Once you hear everyone sounds calm and nice and boring, you keep the station on but don't really listen.

The mist from the coffee in the mug is rising. The sun hits the newspaper you're reading as you stand at the kitchen counter and you feel it on your hand. You think: *That's the feel of the sun on my hand.*

You open the kitchen window and breathe in fresh air — grass, the man next door just mowed. It's fresh and cool. You hear birds. You leave the window open so you can keep hearing them. You think, *I'll put a bird house back there.*

You notice you do not have a hard little ball in your stomach. Your acid glands do not appear to have launched the morning's guerrilla attack on the bagel you're eating. Your heartbeat is not accelerating. You do not have the slight tremor you sometimes get when the phone rings so often it's come to seem like a constant alarm.

The rictus muscles around your mouth are not tightening. You are not frowning. What's happening? Oh — you've returned to life.

You are standing there reading the front page. And the front page does not contain information you must respond to. It contains information other people must respond to — the mayor, say, or the head of the arts committee. You wish them well.

You have only one fear. For a long time you've had a hunch that fear keeps you slim. That anxiety creates a quicker metabolism. That happiness will make you fat.

You think: I'll worry about this next week. Or next month.

You dress in soft clothes. That's what cops and firemen and members of the armed services call not being in uniform. You wear soft old jeans and a thin cotton sweater. They smell of Tide and fabric softener. They feel warm from the dryer. They drape on you light as an oversized glove.

When Karen Hughes worked in the White House she wore hard clothes — wool-blend suits and heels and jewelry and makeup; there were buttons and fasteners and flecks of mascara in the eye. She doesn't have to wear makeup now. She can have a soft face. She can wash her face in Dove foamy cleanser, pat it dry, put on a nice-smelling moisturizer and walk onward into the day.

In that day she can daydream. This is especially important for intelligent people;

it's how they find out what they think. She can walk and go for long drives. This is important for adults as it allows them unconsciously to absorb through their eyes a changing landscape while they think about things big and small, all of which relate to time going by, meaning to a changing of landscapes.

She can not-answer-the phone. Not answering the phone is a great gift in life. When you answer the phone, other humans very often bring you their need. "I need you to listen/know/react/advise." They get you on their agenda.

When you don't answer the phone, you stay on your agenda. Which may or may not be clear but at least is yours.

She can shop. Shopping is a wonderful thing. It's more wonderful if you have money to buy what catches your eye if you want to own it, but it's also fun if you don't have money. It's really wonderful to just sort of walk along the mall and see what your country is selling, buying, offering. You get to see the other people look at and judge your country's products. You can buy a big soft pretzel at a stand and sit on a bench and watch the mothers and daughters buy shoes together. If you sit close enough to hear them you'll be hearing how mothers and daughters talk to each other these days. That's a good thing to know.

Then you can have lunch with friends and bring each other your agendas, which is a word you never use with friends because you don't have to. You know each other so well you don't have an agenda. Or you have one but it's unspoken, shared and simple: It is: We're friends, we help each other through life.

Then you can go home and read a book in a chair outside, or on your bed, with the sunlight streaming in on the comforter. It's good to read. When you read books by people who know things you don't know, or rather who know things you don't know and would benefit intellectually, spiritually or emotionally from knowing, you are giving your brain/soul good nutrients. No one ever got stupider, shallower or worse from doing this.

You can think of dinner. You can make it or order it. You can think of what everyone would enjoy and then try to make sure it'll be good for them too.

You can watch the news and be interested like a normal person by what's going on, as opposed to being interested like an abnormal person — a person who works for a president, say. You can watch TV shows with your son and husband and just enjoy them. You can daydream to them and have uninterrupted thoughts about what's happening in Hollywood and what's happening with people who are 27 and secretly running the country. You can have these thoughts uninterrupted by bells that ring like alarms and agendas that are thrust on you and things you must attend to or the president may suffer.

You can become reacquainted with your country.

You can become reacquainted with the idea of normality.

You can find out how much — or how little — you miss The Great World. You can figure the difference between how much it needed you and how much you needed it.

You can find out how much you need the distractions you used to complain about. You can find out if you were right that you didn't need them.

You can find out what comes in to fill and take the place of the pressure, pleasure and importance you just left. You have to try and make sure that space is filled by better things. But you have to be open-minded, easy and welcoming about the word *better.* It can have broad meanings you didn't expect. . . .

Let me tell you why I'm riffing along. I have a feeling the Hughes Plan is related to Sept. 11. The other day a writer friend e-mailed me and said quick, give me a quote on how Sept. 11 changed your life. She was writing an article and just needed another voice to jump in and give words she could put quote marks around.

I didn't know the answer, or rather I knew a bunch of answers but not one. My friend, however, needed one. So I sat and thought, and then I knew. I wrote back: 'Let me tell you what 9/11 did to me. It made me hungrier for life. It made me feel more tenderly toward it and more grateful. It's all short, even in the worst life is too short, and you want to really feel and experience it and smell it and touch it and thank God for it.'

I realized, again, that Sept. 11 had given me a case of Judith Delouvrier. Judith Delouvrier was a wonderful woman who was my friend; our boys went to school together and she was a fine mother and a happy spirit and she loved her husband and they'd just left their apartment and bought a house in my neighborhood. She had a million plans. She jumped on a plane one summer day and never came back. It was TWA 800.

It was all so impossible, so jarring, so unnatural. And in the months and years after her death, if I was walking along and saw something nice — a pretty baby, a dog, a sweet moment between humans, a beautiful pair of shoes in a store window — I'd feel my usual old mild pleasure. And then I would remember that Judith couldn't see this boring common unremarkable thing. And it made the boring common unremarkable thing seem to me more like a gift, more precious and worthy of attention and appreciation, and even love.

So Sept. 11 did to me what Judith's death did, only deeper and newer. And Karen Hughes, who was with the president that day and the days after, maybe she got a case of Sept. 11 too. And maybe it made some part of her want to be more immersed in life. Or more urgently aware that life is not only what you're doing right this second at the desk, it's also going on out there beyond the desk, it's going by like the wind and if you want to you can step out and feel it.

Why did my friend suggest I already

knew the relation of body and soul? Because he inferred from my essay what I had not even thought of but had nonetheless repeatedly suggested: What you do with your body has an impact on your soul. How you live each day with the circumstances of your daily life has an impact on your soul. Because you *are* a body and a soul, and the reality of one is the reality of the other.

CHAPTER ELEVEN

The Great Shame

Much good happened during John Paul's reign. The Catholic Church grew in Africa and in South and Central America, and the number of Catholics in the world almost doubled, to more than 1.1 billion. The church more than ever came to seem a refuge for the poor and the weak, for the immigrant and the oppressed. This was a beautiful thing to see, and it reflects John Paul's beloved Beatitudes: Blessed are the hungry, the humble.

John Paul was an evangelist who brought the message of the Bible to more than 120 countries. This pilgrim pope brought Christian witness to an unbelieving age, and this, too, was beautiful, for it returned the church to its essential and evangelical roots. Saint Peter walked in sandals telling the world of Christ. John brought the word on Shepherd One.

He canonized 482 saints, more than all the popes in the previous four hundred years combined, and they were a diverse lot, as saints are. Among them was Edith

Stein, a Jewish convert who had become a Carmelite nun, and who died in the gas chambers of Auschwitz. When told she might escape death by proclaiming her Catholicism, she said she should "gain no advantage" from her baptism. "If I cannot share the lot of my brothers and sisters, my life, in a certain sense, is destroyed." At her canonization Mass, which was attended by hundreds of thousands, John Paul said that her life teaches us something we must know to live: "Do not accept anything as the truth if it lacks love. And do not accept anything as love which lacks truth!" There was the Polish priest Maximilian Kolbe, who also died in the gas chambers and was canonized by John Paul; the young father whom Kolbe saved by taking his place in a starvation bunker was old now, but he came to Rome to take part in the celebrations and give witness to a heroic life. John Paul also beatified 1,338 people, again more than all popes combined in the previous four hundred years. In one case, so eager was the pope to honor heroic virtue, he gave the title Venerable to speed the canonization process along. Venerable Pierre Toussaint, born into a Haitian slave family in late-eighteenth-century Haiti, was brought to New York by his owner.

The man died, and his widow, left penniless, collapsed; but with the generosity of a saint, Pierre Toussaint quietly supported her. They had taught him a trade: He was a hairdresser. He went out and made himself the most fashionable and personally admired hair stylist in nineteenth-century Manhattan (among his clients and friends: the wife of Alexander Hamilton). He never let his owner know the extent of his assistance because he did not want her to feel humiliation. When she freed him, he bought the freedom of other slaves. He became a renowned philanthropist and ardent man of God, walking to Mass every day for sixty years (carriage drivers did not stop for blacks) and becoming a force behind the building of Old St. Patrick's church in downtown Manhattan. During a yellow fever epidemic he did not flee the city but stayed, and risked his life to help the sick and dying. He took in the abandoned, fed hungry children — black and white — and felt a special tenderness toward orphans. When he died at age eighty-seven, it was front-page news; he was buried at Old St. Patrick's, which was thronged with the thousands he'd helped. A century and a half later, New York's Cardinal O'Connor asked that Pierre

Toussaint's remains be transferred to St. Patrick's Cathedral, where they have an honored place in a crypt under the altar; he is the only layman ever to receive that honor. The cause for Pierre Toussaint's beatification continues; a miracle is needed. But John Paul kept an eye on his case; and when he last visited New York, he said of Toussaint, "What is so extraordinary about this man? He radiated a most serene and joyful faith, nourished daily by the Eucharist and visits to the Blessed Sacrament. In the face of constant, painful discrimination he understood, as few have understood, the meaning of the words 'Father, forgive them; they do not know what they are doing.' No treasure is as uplifting and transforming as the light of faith."

John Paul was valiant and eloquent in his long battle for the right of all to live and in his fierce resistance to the governments of the West as they moved to push on the materially poor of other countries population controls, including artificial contraception and abortion.

He reached out to Jews, visiting the Great Synagogue of Rome in April of 1986 and asking that Christian-Jewish dialogue become more theological. Christianity's roots are Jewish roots, and Christianity's founders read the Hebrew Bible; we have much to understand and ponder as we consider the mystery of our shared roots and our continuing redemption.

In 2000, during the church's great jubilee year, John Paul decided that at the heart of the celebrations would be a day of penance and pardon, a day in which the church would ask for forgiveness for its historical sins. The church admitted bad actions from the depredations of the Crusades to the horror of the Holocaust. John Paul was blunt: "In certain periods of history, Christians have at times given in to intolerance and have not been faithful to the great commandment of love, sullying in this way the faith of the church. . . ." He humbly asked forgiveness for the church and its people.

What I write here only touches on the most obvious achievements of his papacy. But there were mistakes too, for John Paul was human and his reign was long.

One mistake, in my view, is that he did not move forcefully against the embarrassment of how the Mass is celebrated in the West: the banalization of the liturgy, which is so pervasive that a priest told me recently that saying the flat, ungainly words of Catholic rites is "like chewing cardboard," and the denial of transcendent music and language — the seeming banishment of transcendence itself. In the past thirty years the church has made what was beautiful banal. There has been a pervasive dumbing down: priests who barely know the precepts of their faith, and can barely teach them. Two generations of daffy implementers of Vatican II did this, and John Paul, in my view, seems to have turned his head. It is ironic that the Western church, particularly the American one, is essentially unprepared for the first influx of seekers and potential converts who have begun knocking on the church's door since the extraordinary funeral Mass of John Paul. They watched a week of coverage from Rome, saw the dignity and transcendence of the Church of Rome, heard the sacred music and the smells and bells. This is what they must have it in their heads that they will join. What they're going to get when they enter a church next Sunday in New Jersey is a priest scratching himself distractedly throughout an irrelevant homily, and a woman with a thin voice singing tunelessly as she strums a guitar. It is embarrassing, and yet there is a miracle in it: People come to Mass in spite of it. (I have begun to wonder if Catholics in the pews in America will not soon wonder if Rome is not a bit like Washington: The eternal city allows itself the joys of transcendent tradition and heightened liturgy, and lets the people in the pews elsewhere put up with the banjos while they fill the collection plate, just as those who run the capital city in the United States see to their own needs — the best health care, big staffs — while the rest of us struggle to get what we need and pay for the cost of the government.)

What has been done to the Mass has largely been done in the past thirty years, which is to say on John Paul's watch. Was it his fault? No. Destruction like this comes from ten thousand priests making ten thousand decisions each day. Could he have done more? Yes. Should he have? Yes.

And there was another mistake. It is more famous, it isn't over, and one suspects its root cause is not unconnected to the damage done to the Mass.

John Paul was not famous as a gifted administrator, and he did not spend his time attempting to become an especially sophisticated bureaucrat. It has long been observed that at the beginning of his papacy he felt he had to choose between attempting to control the Curia, the vast bureaucracy that runs the Vatican, and reaching out to the world. He famously chose the latter, and it would be hard to conclude, especially since he took the papacy at roughly the beginning of the mass media age, that his decision was wrong. Because he stood unwaveringly for church teaching, he was called a hard-liner; but he was hardly that. His approach was generally not strict but expansive: His focus was the world.

But in leadership, every decision to move forward here is a decision not to move forward there. And "there" may suffer.

The pope is not a policeman or a prosecutor, and he is not a CEO or a general. Nor is he the local DA. He cannot exert immediate and specific control on all aspects and actors of the church; he cannot direct the actions of the church in every nation of the earth.

But the sex scandals that swept the Catholic Church in America during his reign are, in my view, inescapably part of his legacy, the unhappiest portion. They are part of what he left behind and part of what his successor will have to heal.

They are the great shame of the modern

American church. They did not begin under John Paul's reign but they grew in scope and number during his tenure. By 2003, some twelve hundred Catholic priests in America had been accused of sexual abuse. In the Archdiocese of Boston alone, the Massachusetts attorney general announced that up to a thousand young children had been sexually molested by Catholic priests. By that year, ten American church leaders had resigned, and hundreds of court cases had been brought against the church, which threatened to bankrupt a number of archdioceses.

It is the gravest tragedy in the history of the American church. The scandals had been growing for decades; all the court records suggest it picked up speed in the mid-1960s. Before then, the majority of priests in America who were destructive seemed most often to focus their destructive power on themselves: lost souls, whiskey priests, men who'd lost their faith. They were captured in fiction by, among others, Willa Cather, Graham Greene, and Edwin O'Connor; they were painted as men who thought that they were failures, and yet they were not failures, just human — men of God who had fallen into this pit or that. They struggled.

But the destructive priests who followed them did not confine their damage to themselves. They included among their victims children, parents, and families. They included whole neighborhoods and parishes, and they encompassed generations.

Anyone within the church, sophisticated about the church, privy to its longstanding problems — and that would be just about all of America's current Catholic church leaders — could see the tsunami of woe building and threatening. And they could conclude that when it hit, it would overwhelm the dwellings and lives of the most modest.

I have been struck, reading and researching the scandals, by the number of teenage boys molested and seduced by priests who came from single-parent families. Often their mothers, hoping for some kind of stability, hoping for the influence of a man for their sons to emulate, pressed their confused eleven-year-olds to become altar boys for Father Bill or go on fishing trips with Father Joe. They hoped the priests would serve as role models. Instead, they were predators who felt free to do what they wanted because there was no man in the house to whom they might have to answer. There was only a mother blinded by trust.

Some cases are famous. Many of the earlier ones were centered on the Boston Archdiocese, headed by Cardinal Bernard Law. Among the most well known was that of Father Paul Shanley, who had a history of sexual abuse against boys dating back to 1966 and who ultimately was charged with abusing boys aged six to fifteen from a period of 1979 to 1989. There was the case of the Reverend John Geoghan, charged with sexually molesting scores of boys and girls. His case was settled by the Archdiocese of Boston for a reported ten million dollars. In January 2003 the *Boston Globe* reported that Cardinal Bernard Law had twice responded to charges that Father Geoghan had sexually molested children with recommendations of psychiatric treatment. But when a bishop told Law that local people had complained that Geoghan was acting inappropriately at a swimming pool in Waltham and showing what might be interpreted as a prurient interest in a young boy, Law was apparently not alarmed. In pretrial court testimony Law was asked if it had concerned him that Father Geoghan was in a pool surrounded by children, considering what the church knew about his history. Cardinal Law blandly replied that he just thought, when he heard the complaint, that it was about "proselytizing," as if Geoghan had been talking to the children about the faith. But yes, Law conceded, he had assisted in a 1989 effort to get Geoghan psychiatric treatment that allowed him to continue working at his parish.

The scandals, of course, did not take place only or primarily in the Boston Archdiocese. They occurred all over the country. Perhaps their iconic moment is the Palm Beach story.

In the late 1990s, the bishop of Palm Beach was revealed to have sexually molested several minors. A new bishop was sent in to take his place. He was Bishop Anthony O'Connell, who for almost twenty years had run a high school seminary in Missouri. When Bishop O'Connell was installed, he signed a statement that ringingly condemned the priestly sexual abuses that were cropping up throughout the church. This statement was seen by a man who years before had been one of Bishop O'Connell's seminary students, and whom Bishop O'Connell had sexually molested. The man told his story.

Bishop O'Connell admitted it, more or less. He said he "touched the boy." Then in a full statement to the press, he suggested that his sexual relationship with the boy was meant as "therapy," that it was the fault of the 1970s, that the church then was in the thrall of Masters and Johnson, and that his greatest sin may have been an excess of altruistic zeal — "I've always been a do-gooder." He then suggested that, actually, this was all John Paul's fault for appointing him.

He sounded like Michael Jackson, who famously said, after the first child sex abuse allegations were made against him, "If I'm guilty of anything, it is trying to help all the children in the world."

William F. Buckley, who is no radical on the issue of priestly sex abuse, and has tried to be both patient and truthful on the problem, wrote a column in which he noted that Bishop O'Connell, at his news conference, had asked for prayers for those who supported him. Then the bishop added that he would ask those who were angry at him to "pray for my forgiveness." After reporting this, Buckley noted that he had received a note from his brother Jim about the scandal. James Buckley, the former U.S. senator from New York, and a federal judge, wrote to his brother, "This is an occasion where a papal apology is truly appropriate." He advised that the church should explain that although it continues to love the sinner and hope for reformation and salvation, its overarching responsibility to the faithful requires it "to defrock or otherwise isolate any priest who is guilty of sex abuse."

Who could disagree?

As the scandals broke and became notorious, people would ask my reaction. I was at first shocked, like everyone else. And then angry, like everyone else. People began to ask me if the scandals had shaken my faith. This startled me. It didn't shake my *belief.* How could it? But it certainly left me questioning the operations of the church.

How could the scandal have happened? There are many answers, and many answerers. One that seemed to me wise, and that captured at least a portion of the problem, came from an old monsignor. In the summer of 2003, feeling an anger that had become fury at what so many priests had done, I sought him out. I told the monsignor that I felt swept by resentment, and wanted to admit it, air it, get rid of it, refresh. The monsignor looked down at the floor and said he not only understood, he shared my feelings. It is all disappointing, he said, but he thought there was a reason it had happened in America. He said — I should note that he is an immigrant who came to America twenty-five years ago — "We love our country, but our priests come from our country and from our time. They come from us, are of us. And you know, there is no one 'American people.' We are many people from many places, and we are proud of this. We have all the talent of the world! But we have all the sickness of the world. All the sickness of the world is here."

In his detailed and informed appreciation of John Paul, *Man of the Century*, published in 1997, the journalist and historian Jonathan Kwitny tells this story: In 1992, a brave young Catholic journalist, Jason Berry, wrote *Lead Us Not into Temptation: Catholic Priests and the Sexual Abuse of Children*. It was an indictment of predatory priests and the higher-ups who covered up their crimes. Berry reported that for years the Vatican embassy in Washington had received almost weekly reports of priests who had molested the young. The church had already paid four hundred million dollars in legal settlements. Many guilty priests were allowed to stay on in the priesthood provided that — amazingly enough — they agreed to take the drug Depo-Provera, a female contraceptive thought to dampen the male sex drive. Berry not only detailed case after case of priests who had sexually molested grade school boys, he got his hands on videotapes the priests had taken and were selling.

Berry's book was followed by a *60 Minutes* report. Father Thomas Doyle, a canon lawyer, said that an estimated three thousand of the fifty thousand U.S. priests had sexually abused minors.

Finally, a delegation of U.S. bishops went to Rome. They asked for the right to make "summary judgments" to remove priests who had abused children. But John Paul, Kwitny reported, would not agree. He feared witch hunts, false charges, and unjust oppression, all of which he had seen under Naziism and communism. The bishops said they feared financial disaster from lawsuits. John Paul acknowledged pain for the "victims" but called for compassion. He warned, too, against "sensationalism," and pointed a finger at "the mass media."

So while the American church hierarchy did much wrong, it did not, according to Kwitny's book, receive sufficient help and guidance from the Vatican when it was at last trying to set things right.

Why did John Paul fail to respond adequately in this area? Again, there are as many answers as there are answerers. Some say the scandals were not his fault: He tried to lead the American church toward sanctity, but many of its members — distracted by politics and ideology and conceit, going their own way in the day-to-day — did not and would not listen. Some say John Paul did not respond adequately because by the time the problem reached its height he was too old and too sick to move decisively. Some believe the old man in the Vatican was not consistently given a true, clear picture of the size and scope of the tragedy.

There is, no doubt, truth in all of this. And in this: John Paul was a Pole of another era who simply could not imagine — who had no *category* for — the idea of Catholic priests operating in a kind of protection racket in which they serially molest teenage boys and their superiors engage in a systemic cover-up.

The Poland in which John Paul came of age was a country in which both men and women worshipped; unlike the Irish, and the Italians, the men in Poland didn't leave worship to the women but worshipped along with them. John Paul experienced the priesthood as — and witnessed it every day to *be* — a masculine and manly institution. The pope himself was a hero who had inspired hundreds of young men and women to lives of heroic virtue in the priesthood and the convent. I suspect the very heroism of the pope's life — the courage that his life demanded in facing communism, atheism, Naziism, paganism, the culture of death — tended to blind him to the new menace. The idea of broad, deep sexual decadence infecting the American church — how could that be? How could that be a great struggle? John Paul had seen his fellow Polish priests fight to feed people and hide them from the Gestapo, then save them from the clutches of the commissars. His very concept of the priesthood was as a noble band of brothers. The priests he knew and lived among were great men.

Sin, including sexual sin, is part of

human life, and priests are human beings. They are not virtue machines; they're men, and sometimes they fail. But widespread sexual incontinence and predation, and a church that covered it up and reassigned priests they knew to be serial offenders, endangering more children? Impossible. Not within the categories of known human behavior.

The old Pole could not fully imagine the depth and breadth of the American scandal. And with a background like his, how could he?

Nor was he correct that the American media sensationalized the charges, or promoted them out of animus to the church. I know this in many ways, and one is first-hand. When, in the midnineties, I began to understand what was happening to the church, I went to people in the media and told them this was a growing story. They were always interested, and they were rarely surprised, but they also let me know one way or another that this was just not the sort of material networks and newspapers like to go after. For one thing, the reporting necessary to do the job is extremely time consuming, involving lengthy, labor-intensive, and expensive investigation. If you're lucky enough to get the story and run it, you open yourself to charges of left-wing media bias: "You hate the church, you want to hurt it." Just as important, such reports tended to rouse the resentment of Catholics. And there are more than fifty million Catholic consumers of the news in America. Networks don't want to anger them unless they have to.

News shows and news magazines did feature stories now and then about this abusing priest and that abusing bishop, but they were at least twenty years late in reporting the true scope of the problem.

Not until the *Boston Globe* blew the lid in 2002, with a long and exhaustive series that revealed the persistent shuffling of guilty priests from diocese to diocese in the Boston Archdiocese, allowing them to commit crime after crime, did things begin to change. The *Globe* won a Pulitzer. They deserved the honor.

We all have views on the genesis of the scandals. Here are mine.

The church in America is full of priests who joined the priesthood thirty and forty years ago, when the sexual revolution was in full swing. These were young men who had been produced by a society that was suddenly preoccupied with sex, and with the decisions and discoveries people were making about their sexuality. Some of these men found a place where they would not be forced to decide or declare: the church, a place of high respect that offers positions that require a commitment to living a life of grace and sanctity.

Some went on to become great priests, and many went on to become good ones. Some went on to molest the young. The priesthood became a danger to them, and they became a danger to others.

The sex scandal has been called a pedophilia scandal, but a disproportionate number of abusers targeted and preyed upon pubescent males. Sometimes girls were targeted and sometimes young women, but the primary problem was male homosexuals targeting preteen and early-teenage boys.

The problem of homosexuality in the modern American church has been noted by the liberal Bishop Wilton Gregory, who said in 1992 that it is "an ongoing struggle" to "make sure that the Catholic priesthood is not dominated by homosexual men." The liberal priest and author Father Andrew Greeley has called the homosexual subculture in the church "the Lavender Mafia." The author Michael

Rose, in his book *Goodbye, Good Men — How Catholic Seminaries Turned Away Two Generations of Vocations from the Priesthood*, detailed his experiences with that subculture.

But why would some of these priests have become sexual predators? What made them think they had the right to use the young for their sexual pleasure?

With fewer priests entering the priesthood and more priests aging and retiring, the priests who remained the past thirty years worked hard. They received great sympathy for this from their superiors and parishioners. Some priests became to too high a degree self-regarding. They began to wonder if they didn't have the right to blow off steam, explore their inner nature, get some affection. Some came to act as if they had come to see the church as something that existed to house, employ, and take care of them.

This phenomenon — *I don't belong to a great institution to help others, the great institution exists to help me* — is not unique to the Catholic Church and can be seen now in many institutions. In our public schools, to name one example, there are administrators and teachers who devote most of their time to make sure things go right for them. There is, alas, no union for the kids for whom the schools actually exist. Some school workers forget this, and act as if the schools exist to employ them and see to their rights and needs.

It's a subtle mind shift as to mission, and it can sour and damage large organizations. I believe it happened in the Catholic Church. Malefactors who had abused children were given unhelpful sympathy by their superiors, just as victims were given far too little.

The actions of the abusers and their excusers reflect a profound immaturity, an immaturity that sees children as need-meeting entities and not full humans who have full human rights; an immaturity about even the most routine self-governance and organizational accountability.

It is terrible that victims and families had to turn to the courts to find justice, and terrible, too, that the poor and working families of dioceses throughout the nation will suffer from the cost of the lawsuits, and thus receive less assistance from the church.

The hierarchy of the American church has lost a great deal of its authority. It will be a long time, a generation perhaps, before it gains it back.

But here is the hope: There is a generation of new priests rising. These new priests hate the old ways, the compromises and corruption, and they want to be heroic. They entered the priesthood out of belief and ardor; they went into it, in fact, against the flow of history, with little societal encouragement and few obvious rewards. They went into it, and are going into it, at a time of scandal, when it has never been harder to be a priest. They are the ones who will help right the American church.

More hope: The seminaries and orders that have most embraced evil are dying. Few are joining them. Those that have not embraced evil are growing, and new ones are forming. This is, truly, a happy case of survival of the fittest.

The damage done to the hierarchy may — just may — raise the standing of the clergy who have been largely untouched by the scandal, namely, American nuns. An old nun told me recently that in her view one reason the sex scandals happened is that nuns and priests don't work as closely together anymore. "We weren't there to watch them," she said. Nuns used to be there, watching what was going on in the cardinal's house, and serving as a corrective to the cardinal's thinking. Not so much anymore, and there are fewer nuns, in any case. But if I were one of the men running the church, for public relations reasons alone I'd start elevating the nuns in the area, and conferring with them seriously. (There are some who complain that various convents have also become fairly disturbed in various ways. But not all and not most, and many nuns are truly unknown and unsung heroes. In any case, I think I've noticed a crude and imperfect but serviceable way to judge which women's religious communities work, are constructive and faithful, and which are not. The more old-fashioned the habit, the more Catholic the nun. The more distinctive the dress, the more removed from the world, and the more faithful. A nun in a veil probably prays; a nun in a two-piece suit with nothing on her head but a gray crewcut is somewhat more likely to be thinking of spirit winds and new ways to refer to Jesus as "she.")

Nothing helps the world more than good nuns. And perhaps this is a good time to upgrade their title. They are called sisters when in fact they are mothers, for they mother children in schools and young girls in stress; they mother great institutions like Covenant House in New York and the Sisters of Life in New York. They're as much mothers to the flock as priests are fathers, and even sometimes more. So: not "sister" but "mother."

The American church has learned a terrible and costly lesson. Errant priests can no longer assume they won't be found out, and corrupt bishops can no longer be confident they won't be exposed. The church has an opportunity to renew itself. As the respected churchman Cardinal Avery Dulles said in the spring of 2003, the American church is in urgent need of what he called "far-reaching intellectual, spiritual and moral regeneration." He told a crowd in the Bronx that the church has been swept by confusion, a lack of religious knowledge, dissent, and decline. He slammed "the immoral behavior of Catholics, both lay and clergy," that was "a cause of scandal." Indeed it is. But one senses things are changing, for they must.

I end with "What I Told the Bishops."

In September 2003, Cardinal Theodore McCarrick of Washington; Bishop Wilton Gregory, the head of the U.S. Conference of Catholic Bishops; and a handful of bishops met in Washington with a few dozen Catholic laymen to discuss the future of the church. The official name of the conference was "A Meeting in Support of the Church," but everyone knew the context: the scandals.

Two months before, in July, Cardinal McCarrick and Bishop Gregory, both influential leaders in the church, had held another meeting with laymen, but that meeting was kept secret. They had invited only those who might be characterized as church liberals. The story leaked, as stories do. Many thought that holding a secret meeting to discuss a scandal borne of secrecy was ham handed and tin eared, at best. The cardinal and the bishop were embarrassed. Those often characterized as conservative asked for a similar meeting, and the two men obliged.

I think in some small way the meeting was historic. The non-Catholic public would probably assume that bishops and cardinals frequently talk with conservatives in the church. The non-Catholic American public would probably assume bishops and cardinals *are* the conservatives in the church. But this is not so. Conservatives in the church often feel that they are regarded, and not completely unkindly, as odd folk who perhaps have a third hand growing out of their foreheads. We say, "Please, we must speak more as a church about the meaning of life," and church leaders say, "We may possibly do that after issuing the report on domestic employment policy." We ask the church to teach Catholic doctrine, and they point out that the press doesn't really like the church. We ask them to discuss the pressing issues of the moment, such as cloning — we're entering a world in which industrial fetal farms may grow replacement people for replacement parts — and instead they issue new directives on how it would be better if people sang songs during the Mass after communion and hugged each other instead of shaking hands during the moment of peace.

It's all conversation by non sequitur.

Anyway, Bishop Gregory and Cardinal McCarrick met with conservatives and heard them out for almost an entire day. The conservatives assembled were earnest, informed (it was Princeton's Robert George who warned of a future that could include fetus farms), and direct too.

I had planned to speak on the teaching of Catholic doctrine, which is something the American Catholic Church doesn't really like to do in any depth, at least for the people in the pews. But it seemed to me that earlier speakers had so much to say on so many topics that are crucial and pending that the scandals were given surprisingly short shrift. So I rearranged my speech as others spoke.

There were some central questions that motivated my remarks. Do these men understand the extent and depth of the damage done by the scandal, and is still being done by it? Do they understand the church must move comprehensively to stop it?

To speak of a problem so difficult and yet so delicate, and to do it in front of men who lead the wounded church, and who came up through a system that we now know to have been marked by institutional sickness, seemed to me — well, *delicate* is the best word I can come up with. And so I thought the only fair way to begin was to say that I meant to speak with candor, as one does among friends, that we all love the church and love Christ, and that candor demanded candor about myself too. I said that I spoke from no great moral height, that I was certain I had "the least impressive personal biography in the room," that I was no moral exemplar — far from it. I said I wanted to make this clear because "who we are both as individual people and as a church, who we really are, is at the heart of things."

At this point, I happened to look at Cardinal McCarrick, who was sitting in the front row. He nodded his head and gave me a smile as if to say, "We're all imperfect here; don't worry." It is odd but I *felt* his sweetness. I felt his encouragement.

Then I said my piece.

I told them the scandal was in my view "the worst thing ever to happen in the history of the American church"; I told them they had to stop it now, deal with it fully; that if reports of abusive priests "continue to dribble out over the next two and four and six years, it will be terrible; it could kill the church." I spoke of how terrible it was that just the other day a priest in Maine was finally removed from his parish two years — two years! — after it was revealed that he was one of the priests who had set up the pornographic Web site "St. Sebastian's Angels." I said, "Two years after he was found to be doing what he was doing — and he's still in business!"

I attempted to paint a picture of a man in the suburbs of America, taking his kids to church. He stands in the back in his Gap khaki slacks and his plaid short-sleeved shirt. He stands there holding his three-year-old child. He is there every Sunday; he is loyal and faithful. But afterward — away from church with his friends, at the barbecue or the lunch, he now feels free to say things about the church that only ten years ago would have been shocking. "He thinks the church is largely populated by sexual predators, men whose job now is to look after their own." And then perhaps he adds, "But not my priest." But maybe these days he doesn't say "but not my priest" as often.

And so, I said, we must move. "We use buzzy phrases from the drug wars like zero tolerance" for sexual predators, but maybe we should use words that reflect who we are and where we stand — *defrocking* and *excommunication* being good words that speak of who we are as a church.

I told the bishops and the cardinal that we were a demoralized church, and — I told them this was hard to say — that they, too, must feel demoralized. "Imagine a leader of our church. He became a priest to help humanity, to bring it Christ. And he became a priest and did great work and rose to a position of leadership. And now he is in the meeting where the archdiocese lawyer muscles the single mother who brought suit against the local priest who molested her son after she took the boy to the priest so he could have a good male role model and learn of the greatest male role model, Christ."

So we were demoralized. But there was help. I spoke of the scene in Mel Gibson's movie *The Passion*, which I knew some in the audience had seen in screenings. Mr. Gibson had attempted, obviously, to base his film on the Gospels. But there were a few moments in which his art asserts itself, and he did it his way. There was one scene like this that for me was the great moving moment of the film. The beaten and brutalized Christ falls under the weight of the cross. He's half dead, on his way to Golgotha. When he falls, his mother runs to help him. He looks up at her, blood streaming down his face, and says, "See, Mother, I make all things new again."

I quoted this dialogue to the bishops and the cardinal. And when I said the words that Christ spoke in the film, my voice broke, and for a few seconds I couldn't continue speaking. Cardinal McCarrick looked at me kindly. He has a kind face. I was embarrassed but at the same time, I thought, well, OK.

What choked me was thinking of Jesus. And thinking of how we all want to be new again, and how we can be if we rely on him; but it's so hard. While we believe deep in our hearts, we do not believe, or else we'd all be new again.

Anyway, I regained my composure and concluded my remarks with some hard advice. I said the leaders of the church should now — "tomorrow, first thing" — take the mansions they live in and turn them into schools for children who have nothing, and take the big black cars they ride in and turn them into school buses. I noted that we were meeting across the street from the Hilton, and that it would be good for them to find out where the cleaning women at the Hilton lived and go live there, in a rent-stabilized apartment on the edge of town or in its suburbs. And take the subway to work like other Americans, and talk to the people there. How moved those people would be to see a prince of the church on the subway. "They could talk to you about their problems of faith; they could tell you how hard it is to reconcile the world with their belief and faith, and you could say to them, 'Buddy, ain't it the truth.' "

★ ★ ★

I didn't know if my comments had hit their mark until the meeting was over, when a round and intelligent-looking bishop approached me as I waited on the sidewalk for a cab. I was trying to rush to the airport to make the next shuttle home. He said, "I'd give you a ride but I don't have the limo." I laughed. Now I think perhaps I should have said, "You will."

I was asked privately after the speech if I meant to suggest that the church should divest itself of its beautiful art and cathedrals and paintings and gold filigree. No way. We are not Puritans and not Protestant; Catholicism is, among other things, a sensual faith, and it is our way to love and celebrate the beautiful. Moreover, regular people have as much access to the finery of churches as the rich and powerful. Art is aspirational: It helps us reach. But the princes of our church no longer need to live in mansions in the center of town. Those grand homes were bought and built a century ago, in part so the political leaders of our democracy would understand that the Catholic church had arrived. But they know it now. The point has been made. Cardinals are shepherds, and shepherds don't live in mansions.

In the end, the response from the bishops and the cardinal was not clear to me. They did not refer to any of my points in their remarks, or speak to me afterward. I don't imagine any of the laymen left the meeting with a feeling that great progress had been made in any area. I left with a feeling that some progress may have been made in some area. I did not come away angry, as some did, or depressed. I came away glad that I'd said what I thought needed saying, and feeling somewhat sad and perplexed. *Why would all this be happening? What does God want us to do? And how can flawed and ridiculous people like us help?*

Someone at the meeting quoted the historian Paul Johnson saying some years back to a new Catholic, "Come on in, it's awful!" We all laughed, but you know, I think it was the one thing everyone in the room agreed on.

CHAPTER TWELVE

Life

John Paul spoke a great deal about "the culture of life" and warned against, and asked humanity to resist, "the culture of death." What did this mean?

He had seen a lot of death in his time. He came of age during the most killing century in the history of mankind, had lost friends in the war; and by the time he was in his early twenties, he had lost everyone who mattered to him, all of his family. Death had robbed him of much. But the immediate culture in which John Paul was raised, the culture of the working- and middle-class Catholics of Poland, loved and valued life. When he was a boy, he said, women were "elevated" and "respected." There was no abortion; the sick were allowed to live until their bodies died, as were the old. People knew in their bones that God actually made us, that we are actually his children, and so we were by definition special, precious.

So that is where he started, with that knowledge.

During his papacy he came to see which way the world was growing. More liberation but less fully experienced liberty; more modernity, less coherence. More media and more encouragement of violence; more separating of sexuality and love, of sexuality and marriage.

He did what he tended to do: He thought about what was happening and then he wrote, and then he spoke. What he published in March 1995 was a great encyclical, his eleventh, "The Gospel of Life." And in it he was as clear as crystal about abortion, euthanasia, and the inherent dignity of a human life. It is here that he first uses the phrase "the culture of death."

What is it? It is a culture that sees moral wrongs as human rights, that sees the ending of human life in the womb as a legitimate and protected choice, or the ending of a feeble life as acceptable, as practical and even humane. But human beings are not to be judged as "useful" or "useless." A society that does not hold human life high and inviolable summons its own destruction. The liberal democracies are courting their death. And though the world's modern liberal democracies have laws that, to varying degrees make abortion legal, and pursue laws that will make euthanasia legal, "Abortion and euthanasia are . . . crimes which no human law can claim to legitimize. There is no obligation in conscience to obey such laws; instead, there is a grave and clear obligation to oppose them by conscientious objection."

Abortion, the pope declares, is gravely immoral because it is the deliberate taking of innocent human life. Likewise, euthanasia is immoral. Both deny human "solidarity." Both are at odds with the respect and protection we owe our brothers and sisters in life. The culture of death "is actively fostered by powerful cultural, economic, and political currents that encourage a . . . society excessively concerned with efficiency. . . . A person who because of illness, handicap, or, more simply, just by existing, compromises the well-being or life-style of those who are more favored, tends to be looked upon as an enemy to be resisted or eliminated."

He is saying all have a right to life. Babies in the womb have a right to be alive, be born, and walk the earth. We all of us have a right to be sick, damaged, unwell. We don't have to be perfect to merit life; we can be imperfect, ungainly. We all have a right to be old if we are given to grow old. These circumstances — innocent vulnerability, illness, old age — are normal, not unusual or extraordinary, not a threat to the enjoyment of life but part of life on earth, part of its tapestry, and an expression of God's wishes: that we live.

He is also saying that once you go down the road where some unfortunate people can be put to death, you won't know where the journey will end. Once you decide some lives are not worth living or not important, then you have journeyed to a new place where you decide who gets to live and who dies. This is a place that leaves you coarsened, that leaves your conscience cruder, rougher, less open to love and its appeals. Once you get there, your next stop, or the one after that, is genocide, or the careless killings that mark our age — or the gas chambers. Don't go down that road, John Paul says. Get off that road; get off that bus. It leads to no good place. "The right to life," he later said, "means the right to be born and then continue to live until one's natural end." That — the natural end — should be left to God.

The pope's views here were uncompromising, but they also showed an attentiveness to the realities of life as lived in the modern world. Extraordinary measures in medical treatment for the ill in hospitals, for instance, are not by any means always called for. If the patient is dying, is the victim of a fatal illness, for instance, and if the procedures are "disproportionate to any expected results," treatment can legitimately be discontinued. Likewise, drugs and pain relievers that may turn out to shorten a life but are intended simply to alleviate pain are legitimate.

The death penalty, though, is barely so. John Paul, who had seen up close the wild state abuse of the power to kill, came out against the death penalty in almost all cases. The Catholic Church had long held that capital punishment was a legal way for society to attempt to defend itself and to deter crime. John Paul said capital punishment should be used for societal defense only in cases of "absolute necessity." He said prisons have come a long way in protecting society. Then he added that cases in which the death penalty is absolutely necessary were "very rare" if not "practically nonexistent."

Five years later, in his book of interviews, the best-selling *Crossing the Threshold of Hope*, John Paul, having been asked again about abortion, took an interesting turn in his conversation. "It is necessary to recognize," he said, "that . . . we are witnessing true human tragedies. Often *the woman is the victim of male selfishness,* in the sense that the man, who has contributed to the conception of the new life, does not want to be burdened with it and leaves the responsibility to the woman, as if it were 'her fault' alone." The italics are his.

He continued, "So, precisely when the woman most needs the man's support, he proves to be a cynical egotist, capable of exploiting her affection or weakness, yet stubbornly resistant to any sense of responsibility for his own action. These are problems that are well know not only in confessionals, but also in courts throughout the world and, more and more these days, in courts that deal with minors."

It is not enough to reject "pro choice"; we must "become courageously 'pro woman,' promoting a choice that is truly in favor of women." Women pay the highest price for "the suppression of the life of the child who has been conceived." The only "honest stance" for society, for all of us, is a new and "radical solidarity" with women in this drama.

Here I would note that John Paul, in asserting these truths, was at odds with the spirit of the age in which he lived. Catholics of the West routinely said in polls that they did not accept church teaching — his teaching — on abortion, on the sanctity of life. And John Paul knew this. He knew especially that the intellectual class of the West would not take seriously his pronouncements. But he said them again and again, at risk of being accused of being obsessed — he denied it, saying he was addressing, as a human being and a leader, the "fundamental" human "imperative" to protect other humans who are "incapable of defending themselves."

In his last book, published the year of his death, John Paul again addressed what he was up to. He said he knew what he was fighting: the smooth carriers and encouragers of death, the ones who come forward in the name of tolerance but whose fruits are sadness and woe. We must fight, he said. We must speak. "Silence in the presence of the enemies of a cause encourages them. Fear in an apostle is the principal ally of the enemies of the cause. 'Use fear to enforce silence' is the first goal in the strategy of the wicked. The terror used in all dictatorships depends on the fearfulness of apostles. Silence possesses apostolic eloquence only when it does not turn its face away from those who strike it. So it was in the case of Christ's silence."

So now we know it was strategy. And strategy that, of course, took courage. It took a personal decision to put his own reputation and popularity second, his dislike of criticism second, and his commitment to tell the truth first, always. He did this. And here's the funny thing. People may not say they notice, and people may say they admire; they may not say they agree with you, and they may not say they know you are holding high the most important truths that can be spoken. But they are always watching, and thinking. And at the end, those crowds who engulfed Rome when he died — maybe they were responding to the old man's courage, paying homage to it, and declaring that it had won their love and gratitude. Someone has to hold high the truth. And when someone does we know, somewhere deep down. We know.

CHAPTER THIRTEEN

The Day Draws Near

In the spring of 2003, on March 21st, John Paul held an audience and departed from his text. Lately he had often been departing from his text. But this day it was startling, for he bluntly told the gathered crowd in St. Peter's Square that "the day is drawing near." He said soon he would face his maker and have to "account" for his life.

This gave some in the crowd, and some who would later read his comments, a bit of a shudder. *If he is worried about his accounts, how worried should I be?* But the pope didn't seem worried. He just seemed serious. It seemed to me, when I read the story and saw the pictures of the event days later, that he was preparing people for his leaving. This is something he'd taken to doing a lot.

Why prepare them at all? Previous popes had aged and bowed to illness without telling people that they were leaving.

What was he up to? What did he want us to know?

★ ★ ★

Endings were on his mind. A few weeks before, on Saturday, March 1st, John Paul had done something else surprising. He spoke in public to strangers about his past. He did it in a strong voice, ad-libbing, and he seemed to have a good time. When his aides tried to shuffle him off, he moved his head as if to say, "My handlers want me to move on, but I'm not ready just yet."

It was a Vatican meeting with seminarians from throughout the world who were studying for the priesthood. The pope had completed a standard address in which he told the young men it would take courage for them to fully embrace their vocation. Then he spoke spontaneously about his youth in Poland during World War II. He put down his prepared speech and told the young seminarians what it was like for him to study, in secret and under pain of arrest or death, for the priesthood.

That place and that time, Poland, circa 1939 to 1945, can perhaps best be understood as the funnel through which the twentieth century poured its woes. The pope and his nation had lived through a brutal Nazi invasion in 1939, when he was still a teenager. Throughout much of the occupation that followed, the troops of the

Soviet Union waited, massed, on the shores of the Vistula River, ready to descend when the day came that the Nazis would be defeated and withdraw. The people of Poland were as abused as any in history — hounded, starved, imprisoned, murdered, sent to death camps. The pope was then a young chemical factory worker studying for the priesthood in a secret seminary. He and the good priests who taught him would have been killed if they had been discovered. The Nazis did not want more Catholic priests, nor did the Soviets.

John Paul had spoken of those years to biographers, but he didn't do it often in public and he hadn't done so in a long time. The fact that he did in the spring of 2003, spontaneously, in St. Peter's Square, and with what the Associated Press later called "a vigor now rarely seen in public," seemed meaningful.

For ten minutes the pope told the seminarians arrayed before him of his youth. He felt called to the priesthood, he said, and so he took instruction in the cellar of a nearby church. But he continued to work his shifts at the factory, and it was difficult for him. But, said the pope, his coworkers, rough Polish men living lives as stressed as his own, helped him with his religious education by trading shifts and occasionally covering for him, at their peril. He learned his faith "in those terrible years of war and clandestinity," he told the crowd.

He told them how much he owed his co-workers. He brought his books to the factory, and they helped him keep his studies secret. In those days, he was studying Christian metaphysics. His reading gave him "a new vision of the world, a new, profound penetration of reality."

Then he told the crowd what he thought of it all now, so many years later. He said he thanked God for those days. "I thank the Lord who gave me this extraordinary experience and who let me speak of this experience as a clandestine seminarian to seminarians in Rome after more than 50 years." He thanked God for the pain that had deepened his understanding of life, and that had been followed by joy.

One of his aides came forward and whispered in his ear, and John Paul laughed and told the young men gathered before him that he had to give them their blessing now. There were things to do, a schedule to be maintained. The young seminarians left, departing emotionally, moved by what the pope had said to them, and how he had said it.

★ ★ ★

At this time, it turned out the pope had also been writing poetry again. He had been a published poet before the papacy, but he hadn't written much poetry since, or any that anyone knew of. Now all of a sudden we learned that he had returned to writing in the summer of 2002, and his latest poems were published in the spring of 2003.

There was an autumnal quality to the work. The pope had referred in private meetings in the previous few years to his passing, but even sophisticated Vatican observers were taken aback by the long poem he had written in Castel Gandolfo.

It was called "Roman Triptych." In the second part of the poem, "Meditations on the Book of Genesis at the Threshold of the Sistine Chapel," John Paul reflected on the day he was elected pope by the cardinals of the church. He referred to the inevitable choosing of his successor. He said the great cardinals of the church would be called from each corner of the earth and would come together once again, under the frescoes of Michelangelo, beneath his masterpieces *Creation* and *The Last Judgment*. In the poem the pope imagines the day when his successor is chosen:

So it will be again, when the need arises
    after my death.
Michaelangelo's vision must then speak
    to them. . . .
They will find themselves between the
    Beginning and the End.
Between the day of Creation and the
    Day of Judgment.
It is given to man once to die, and after
    that the judgment.

He was speaking both literally and meta-phorically — the College of Cardinals does meet under Michelangelo's great frescoes when a pope dies — but the poem also made one curious. What did Michelangelo's vision "speak" to John Paul when he was the cardinal from Kraków and attending two papal enclaves, the one that picked John Paul I and the one that picked him? What thoughts had he had as he looked up?

In the days immediately before and after his speech to the seminarians, John Paul was busy. His actions suggested his thoughts continued to be on world conflict, but not the conflicts of the past, in his homeland. What seemed to press on him now were the conflicts that were roiling the world in his old age.

He had launched a campaign to include references to the reality of God in the new proposed constitution of the European Union, asking that it include an acknowledgment of the role of the Christian church on the continent of Europe since the very death of Christ. He reached out for an ally in the Greek Orthodox archbishop Christodoulos of Athens, telling him that day by day, to his dismay, Europe was growing "all the more worldly and secular and continues to distance itself from basic Christian values." He received the Orthodox archbishop's support. John Paul reached out to Serbian Orthodox leaders; they, too, supported him, agreeing it was wrong to exclude from new Europe's founding documents the crucial importance of faith in the continent's history. He met with British prime minister Tony Blair in a private audience in which he told Blair, whose wife and children are Catholic, and who has long been rumored to be considering joining the Roman church, that Christianity must not be ignored or forgotten in the EU constitution. But it appeared John Paul was fighting a losing battle. The bureaucrats of Brussels, where the EU constitution was being drafted, and their like-minded diplomatic associates in the member states of the EU, were not interested in including references to God in their great document.

This must have been painful for John Paul, painful in itself and painful in what it represented: the sense, documented by statistics on Mass attendance, churchgoing, church involvement, religious practice and lifestyle, that Catholic Europe, during John Paul's reign, had become post-Christian Europe. The great Catholic writer Hilaire Belloc had said, at the beginning of the twentieth century, "Europe is the faith and the faith is Europe." That was actually still true then. It is not true now. You can walk the streets of Paris at Christmastime, as I have, and you wouldn't know it was a great Catholic holiday if you didn't have a calendar. You can walk the streets of Dublin — Dublin! — on a Sunday morning and see more people at brunch than in church. There are those who argue that this is John Paul's fault, or at least responsibility. In American conservative Catholic circles they say, "On his watch we lost Europe." But it wasn't his fault. It was his grief.

And I wonder what he would have thought, how he would have reacted, if he had lived two months longer and seen, in the late spring of 2005, the people of France and of the Netherlands amaze the world by voting against the European constitution. There is no sign they did it for reasons the pope would have found especially heartening, and yet he had perhaps contributed to an on-the-ground sense in Europe that the new proposed constitution was not a plus.

To my mind, two huge things happened to Europe in the twentieth century that changed its very essence — its shared culture, its assumptions, its understanding of life. The first was the cataclysm of World War I, which robbed Western Europe of a generation of young men. They had marched out under flags and crucifixes and had never come back, and that huge and historic trauma broke something in Europe's spirit that has not been healed. When you lose a generation, you lose a future — and you lose hope. Cynicism settled in, and sourness about great projects and their cost. France was a brave country until the end of World War I, and then they never wanted to fight for anything ever again. Then World War II — more carnage and ruin, and genocide.

The second thing that happened to Europe took place later in the twentieth century. It was the rise of modernity, of broad, growing, and then historic affluence; the rise of the material world and its distractions and glittering prizes; the possibility of living lives that were in central ways more detached from life, from its sunrise demands, muddy miseries, and plain joys; the rise of the isms, of socialism, communism, Naziism, capitalism; the spread of Freudianism, the seeing of man as a psychological rather than a spiritual being. Any one of these would tend to detach some men from their faith; the confluence of all of them in roughly a fifty-year period, and after the trauma of two world wars, destabilized the Continent. And now came changing demographic patterns: Europeans, no longer Catholic, were not having enough children to replace themselves. The people of more crowded and less affluent Islam began coming in, and have been coming in for thirty years. And they are having babies.

Could John Paul have changed all this? Could he have changed any of it? How? Ultimately people change themselves. They have freedom. You cannot force them to change their minds. What John Paul could do is precisely what he did: He personally took the word of Jesus Christ compellingly through the streets of these countries; he wrote to them; he spoke to the people over the heads of the media and the heads of the culture, if you will, urging that they consider God, embrace God, live as God asks. He prayed for them. He asked God to change their hearts. And he must have been frustrated by them, for there was always the sense with John Paul when he spoke to the rich, when he spoke to the wealthy nations, that they did not, of all the people in the world, have the most direct access to his heart. He grew up in a country that was poor, that was bullied, and that was occupied by foreign armies. They didn't have religious freedom through most of his life. Didn't luxurious Western Europe understand what a gift it was to be able to practice your faith in public? Didn't they understand that others had fought for that gift and secured it for them?

Poland knew how to suffer. Poland knew how to pray. So does suffering Africa, so do the poor of the Americas and the Philippines. People who are so lucky they don't even think they have to pray — how could John Paul have not been frustrated by them?

★ ★ ★

And yet, for all this, something happened at the beginning of the twenty-first century that showed us a different picture and suggested that maybe, just maybe, John Paul was right in his decision to carry the Gospel. It was the first great moment of the twenty-first century, and it occurred when John Paul died, at his funeral. Europe came. Europe took to the streets. Millions of pilgrims spontaneously came to his funeral. You could see the signs they held as they stood in the famous line that stretched from St. Peter's across the river Tiber — signs that said Poland, England, France, Italy, Ireland. You could see it by the flags they waved. You could see it when, at the funeral, the crowd burst into applause more than a dozen times, and chanted "The Great, The Great." That was Europe rising up, and coming, and weeping. That was Europe showing that there may be more going on in the European heart right now than statistics can express, or reflect.

One sensed that Europeans may, just may, have come back from that funeral a newly heartened people.

CHAPTER FOURTEEN

Beatification

One bright afternoon in October 2003, I got a call inviting me to be a member of the U.S. delegation to the ceremonies commemorating the twenty-fifth anniversary of John Paul's papacy, which would include a beatification ceremony for Mother Teresa, who was on her way to becoming a saint. The caller, in the president's Office of Public Liaison, could not possibly have understood what a gift this was and what it would mean to me. It gave me one of the greatest moments of my life, a moment that was an accident, a challenge, and a blessing.

Two Emmy Award–winning filmmakers, Ann and Jeanette Petrie, had labored for years on a film about the life and death of Mother Teresa. The Vatican included it in their official program on the occasion of the beatification. The film would make its world premiere in the Paul VI Audience Hall, with Mother Teresa's successor present, and her nuns from throughout the world and many foreign delegations.

The day I arrived in Rome, the man who

was to introduce the film called to say he had to cancel his appearance. The producers tracked me down in my hotel room and asked if I would take his place. I felt uncomfortable: I had had no association with Mother Teresa and had already, after only a day in Rome, bumped into a number of people who seemed to me better choices. I suggested some of them. But the producers, who had watched Mother Teresa closely and perhaps learned how to gently get what they felt they needed, said no, thank you, we need your help. So I agreed.

I had met Mother Teresa once, in 1984, when she was given, by President Reagan, the Medal of Freedom. That spring day I was so excited to know a saint was in the building, but I couldn't get into the ceremony at which she was given her award. I found out the route she would take when she left the White House, however, and I waited there hoping she would come by. She did, in her white habit with the dark blue trim and an old dark blue cardigan. She came toward me, down a walkway where I was standing. She was carrying a handful of blue and white pamphlets. She put one in my hand. I said, "Thank you, thank you, Mother." And then she looked at me and said, "Luff Gott!" *Love God.* And walked on, with a little bevy of nuns fluttering happily behind her.

Today that pamphlet is framed and on the wall of my office. It contains a drawing of Christ on the cross, and a poem by Mother Teresa.

Jesus is the Unwanted — to be wanted.
Jesus is the Leper —
    to wash his wounds.
Jesus is the Beggar —
    to give him a smile.
Jesus is the Drunkard —
    to listen to him.
Jesus is the Mental — to protect him.
Jesus is the Little One —
    to embrace him.
Jesus is the Blind — to lead him.
Jesus is the Dumb — to speak for him.
Jesus is the Crippled —
    to walk with him.
Jesus is the Drug Addict —
    to befriend him.
Jesus is the Prostitute — to remove
    from danger and befriend.
Jesus is the Prisoner — to be visited.
Jesus is the Old — to be served.

I had never heard words quite like

that — Jesus is the prostitute; Jesus is the leper. It was reorienting in some way. Meeting Mother that day was one of the most exciting things that had ever happened to me, and after she left me I did something childish. I jumped up and clicked my high heels.

Ten years later I saw Mother Teresa again, on February 3, 1994, at the National Prayer Breakfast in Washington, at the Hilton Hotel, where she was the main speaker. And there I saw her again do something that I would never forget. She told the entire gathered Washington establishment — President Clinton and the first lady, Vice President Gore and Tipper, most every senator and congressman in town — that abortion is the beginning of the end of a society. "[I]f we accept that the mother can kill even her own child, how can we tell other people not to kill one another? . . . Any country that accepts abortion is not teaching its people to love one another but to use any violence to get what they want. That is why the greatest destroyer of love and peace is abortion."

These words were followed by silence, and then applause that erupted on one side of the hall and finally rocked the ballroom. The president and the first lady, the vice president and his wife, the senators and congressmen had not been lectured in this way in a very long time, if ever. The Clintons in particular sat unmoving, staring straight ahead like seated figures in Madame Tussaud's. But Mother Teresa was not done. "I know that couples have to plan their family," she said, "and for that there is natural family planning. The way to plan the family is natural family planning, not contraception. In destroying the power of giving life or loving through contraception, a husband or wife is doing something to self. This turns the attention to self, and so it destroys the gift of love in him and her. . . . Once that living love is destroyed by contraception, abortion follows very easily. That's why I never give a child to a family that has used contraception, because if the mother has destroyed the power of loving, how will she love my child?"

No one had said the word *contraception* in public in Washington since perhaps 1958. The crowd was taken aback — a U.S. senator turned to his wife at the end and said, "Is my jaw up yet?" — but moved too, and when Mother Teresa left, they took to their feet and applauded for a long time.

★ ★ ★

So I'd seen her and loved her but had no idea what I'd say about her. I had two days to think about it.

In the meantime, there were masses for John Paul and Mother Teresa, and there was the morning of her beatification, which took place at an open-air Mass in St. Peter's Square. The American delegation sat near where John Paul's cedar casket would rest seventeen months later, in the sunny square in front of the Vatican.

It was that night, the night of the beatification Mass, that I was to speak at the Paul VI Audience Hall. I was told that I was the first woman ever to make a speech from the papal stage. Women had been on that stage to sing or perform or play an instrument with a great symphony, but none had given a speech there. I think I was told this in part to underscore the obvious: This is serious, don't do anything inappropriate. And don't try to be amusing. Which only intensified my nerves.

I had not been able, in two days, to think of anything about Mother Teresa that seemed good enough to say, that seemed original or worthy of a saint. The morning of her beatification I awoke from a fitful sleep and realized that although some problems are just problems, some are gifts. I was surrounded by members of the American delegation who had known her and watched her for years. And they were brilliant. The secret of what should be said must reside within them. So at a reception at the home of the American ambassador to the Vatican, Jim Nicholson, I went from member to member and asked for their thoughts.

Sister Mary Rose McGeady, of Covenant House in New York City, told me, "Mother Teresa was a living gospel. She did not have to preach it in words, she preached through her *behavior.* She made a decision about her vocation on a train ride; she had an inspiration and she responded to it. That is such an example for *women,* who feel cast in a role sometimes, but who can *react to inspiration.* She got this idea that God was calling her to the poorest of the poor. And she brought her students, which means she was already, even young, being an example to women."

As the wheelchair-bound Sister Mary Rose said those last words, she tapped her cane on the floor for emphasis.

Harvard Law School's warm-hearted Mary Ann Glendon offered: "I can't help thinking about what we learned after her death, from her papers and diaries. We learn that from the moment of her 'second calling' — the momentous decision — that she entered this period of terrible spiritual desolation. We tend to think that if we were experiencing a decline of our spirituality — distracted, bored in Mass — that something is wrong with us. But to know one of our greatest saints experienced this! And she came to experience it as a gift, in the sense that it allowed her to participate in the suffering of Christ on the cross. 'My God, why have you forsaken me?' When Mother Teresa could not encounter Christ in her prayer life, she began to encounter him in the sick and the suffering and the poorest of the poor. I think it's a great blessing for us that this part of her life has been revealed to us — just as the Holy Father teaches us to deal with physical infirmities, Mother Teresa teaches us how to deal with spiritual infirmities."

And this point, after speaking to Mary Ann and Sister Mary Rose, I knew I was doing the right thing. They were writing my speech for me. They were meant to give it, and give it they would, though I would speak it.

Then I saw Columba Bush, Mrs. Jeb Bush, the head of our delegation as first lady of Florida and representative of the Bush family. She told me, "I think Mother Teresa was and still is a great inspiration. She made a very great difference in my life. I met her in Miami twenty-five years ago. I have been in some of her homes in Mexico. She is an inspiration. What does her life mean? That we should care for each other."

Then I spoke to Mother Agnes, superior general of the Sisters of Life in Yonkers, New York. She said, "What comes to mind is Mother Teresa's humility. By that I mean that she let God take over completely. And I think we witnessed that today in St. Peter's Square; because she was such a fine instrument of God she touched millions of lives — as only God can. And she lives on in the smiling faces of her sisters."

I met with Jim Towey, deputy assistant to the president of the United States for faith-based initiatives. Jim has a wonderful story. He had worked for two years with the Missionaries of Charity with Mother Teresa and was thinking of the priesthood. He found in time that his real calling was to fatherhood, husbandhood, family. He met a beautiful young woman who also worked with Mother. The nuns thought it a good match, as did Mother, who not only urged them to marry but suggested a wedding date. Mother's nuns sang at the wedding. And now they have five children, and Jim works in the White House.

When I asked Jim Towey what he would say about Mother Teresa, he said, "She was a mother. She was the most Mary-like person since Mary. She did motherly things. She was like that in her thirties. They were calling her Mother Teresa when she was twenty-seven. She was virgin and mother to the world."

Then I spoke to the writer and editor Kate O'Beirne, of *National Review*. She said, "How about our Holy Father doing this when he is so handicapped and ill — to honor the woman who gave her life to the handicapped and ill. It is a terribly important day for women. There was the church hierarchy gathered together in St. Peter's Square and looking up at this portrait of this simple, smiling, brilliant woman. Mother Teresa — she would never settle for equality. It's all about holiness."

And finally I spoke to Mary Ellen Bork, author and lecturer and herself a former nun. She told me, "I was thinking about the theme of our whole visit here. Jesus speaks to us through the humanity he took.

He could have just stayed in heaven but he chose to have a body, to be human. Mother Teresa saw God in the *suffering* of *humanity.* There is something Mother says to the church about loving God and expressing that love through our humanity. Today's Mass made you think about heaven. A half million people praying, all of us looking up. For two thousand years we've been doing this, raising people up. It's so human, raising up these humans."

And so I had my speech. Someone called out to me, "You know what they say: 'Go where the Holy Spirit takes you. But make sure to get there in three minutes.'"

When I walked into the great gathering in the cavernous Paul VI Audience Hall, I was taken aback. There were thousands there, from every country represented in Rome, and they were excited. Word of the excellence of the film had spread. There was a group of dozens of cardinals and bishops up front.

I walked up onto the stage. There was no podium, just two long-necked microphones. One arched toward me, the other toward Archbishop John Foley, who had been asked to speak as my interpreter. He is an American who speaks Italian. Between my one language and his talent, we'd be able to communicate to most though not all of the thousands assembled.

I introduced myself, thanked everyone for coming, and spoke of the beatification that morning. "All the reports said there would be rain, heavy rain. It would take a miracle for the sun to come out. Did you see the sun today?" Yes, they said. "Do you think it was Mother's first beatification miracle?" They cheered.

Archbishop Foley was an excellent translator, but it was odd to have a translator. I'd never had one before. He looked like a jolly man. He looked as if he would enjoy humor.

"You see that I have a kind and talented translator in Archbishop Foley," I said. He translated this but began to laugh as he called himself "talented," which delighted the crowd. Then I said, "Archbishop Foley is also a very handsome man, isn't he?"

After a second's pause half the crowd burst into laughter, the nuns cheered, and Foley blushed. I looked at him innocently and said, "You forgot the translation." He intoned, in Italian, "Archbishop Foley is a handsome man." Now all the crowd laughed, especially the cardinals and archbishops, and Archbishop Foley picked the skullcap off his head to show us how high his blush had gone.

I spoke of the ceremony all of us had witnessed that morning. "As I experienced the beatification of Mother Teresa, and the Mass in St. Peter's Square, and saw the pope, John Paul the Great, I felt we were all loving two saints today, Mother Teresa and John Paul. And as I watched it all with the American delegation, another member leaned over and said, 'I am not good enough to be here.' She felt she wasn't a good enough Catholic to be here. When she said it, I thought, *Mother Teresa would like that.* She would like my friend's humility. She would like it because it speaks of our sometimes messy but authentic and God-given humanity."

I said that most of the audience would not necessarily know how Americans feel and felt about Mother, but I had asked members of the American delegation to share with me their thoughts, and I wanted to share them.

I read the words of Mary Ann Glendon, and Sister Mary Rose, and Mother Agnes, and Columba Bush, and Jim Towey, and Mary Ellen Bork.

Everyone listened closely. Big good things were being said. And then, I found out later, a little miracle of a moment happened. When I read the words of Mother Agnes of the Sisters of Life — "She let God take over completely . . . she was such a fine instrument of God — she touched millions of lives as only God can" — when I read those words, just at the moment I read them, Mother Agnes, who had been called to meetings near the Vatican, was hurriedly crossing St. Peter's Square on her way back to her room. In St. Peter's Square they had set up huge Jumbotrons for the hundreds of thousands of pilgrims who had come to take part in Mother Teresa's beatification. They were watching what was happening in Paul VI Audience Hall. And just as Mother Agnes was walking along, the wind blowing her habit, wondering how I'd done in my speech, she heard my voice. And she looked up and saw my face on the Jumbotron as I said the words, "As a wonderful member of our delegation, Mother Agnes of the Sisters of Life pointed out, humility is something we associate with Mother Teresa . . ."

Mother Agnes would later find me and tell me of her moment, being alone and tired and walking through St. Peter's Square and suddenly hearing her name fill the square . . .

I don't know why that hit me as such a big thing, but it did, and Mother Agnes and I became friends. (One day months later, the producers of the game show *Jeopardy!* called and asked if I'd like to be on their show in which Washington people play in order to raise funds for a group or charity. I called Mother Agnes and said that if her convent would pray for me, I would play for them. And pray they did, and the following month the Sisters of Life received a check in the amount of twenty thousand dollars from the producers of *Jeopardy!*, my modest winnings as the person who came in second. There is a great unseen circularity in life, and we are all interacting with the people we are supposed to help and be helped by.)

Anyway, my speech was done and the audience was generous, and the movie about Mother Teresa was intelligent and moving. It was a good night.

After that night, the members of the delegation came together and talked about what had been the highlights. I already knew.

It was the moment in the Scavi — the excavation site deep down in the bottom of St. Peter's, where we had been taken to see the bones of St. Peter. His bones lie in a little hole in a little wall, in plastic. The priest who took our delegation down had begun to pray as we looked at the bones of the first pope, and we all spontaneously got down on our knees and prayed together.

It was the moment when Columba Bush spontaneously went to her knees and prayed alone early in the morning as we walked silently through St. Peter's Basilica.

It was the moment when, as we walked through the empty Basilica one morning, shafts of morning sun came through the high windows and poured onto the empty marble floor.

It was Cardinal Baum's face — he is a gentle old man, eighty-eight years old, who walks with a cane and speaks with a low thin voice. He has round eyes and a soft face and poreless skin. If angels grow old, they must look like this. He talked to me about the meaning of suffering, and then asked for his cane and asked me to help him rise.

It was seeing the offering of the gifts at the pope's twenty-fifth anniversary Mass. There, walking toward the pope, was a beautiful young woman in full Mexican folk dress. As a little child, five or so, she had been abandoned on the streets of Mexico City. She was put in an orphanage. Mother Teresa came to visit. The little girl had attached herself and followed Mother Teresa through the halls. And Mother had laughed; and through a cascade of circumstances, the child was adopted by an American woman and had come to live in America, where she was given the best schooling then available for Down syndrome children. Now here she was at the Mass beatifying the mother she had trailed as a child. She was a vibrant, smiling young woman. When she had given to the pope her offering, she walked past us, and she saw among us her godfather, Jim Towey. He made a hand gesture. So did she. It was the sign language symbol for *love.* And Jim Towey wept, and then told me the story.

It was the moment in the beatification Mass for Mother Teresa when the male choir arrayed in front of St. Peter's sang with deep voices, "Kyrie Eleison." Lord, have mercy. And the whole square full of people, half a million pilgrims come to honor Mother, was quiet, completely quiet. The sound of the repeated "Kyrie Eleison" echoed like a lost choir. It echoed against the Bernini colonnade, echoed against the stone and marble of St. Peter's Square and came back to us. Those stones, these columns, that obelisk — the obelisk from Nero's circus, now topped with a crucifix, the last thing St. Peter is said to have seen before he died — those stones and marbles had over the years absorbed and echoed the sound of many prayers, many choirs. As a church, we have been doing this for a long time, for fifteen hundred years in this square, and the stones and columns have witnessed and absorbed so much. And now today at this moment the old church raises up and beatifies a human being, a small frail woman tough as wire, a flawed and imperfect human being. And that is a wonderful thing for a church to do.

There were other moments for me, other memories that were not so spiritual and not so happy. I saw more cardinals and bishops of the American church than I ever had, and from talking to them, I felt that they still did not understand the impact on the laity and on the reputation of the church and its American leaders that the sex abuse scandals had had. I was taken aback to see what a great figure of respect in the Vatican Cardinal Law still is.

He was up front at the pope's anniversary Mass and the pope's audience, and he dominated animated clusters in the American ambassador's house. At one point I was sitting with Cardinal Baum, at a table with Sister Mary Rose of Covenant House and various bishops. Cardinal Law joined us, and talked about his recent trip to the Holy Land. As he spoke, I felt I saw his suffering. He was so eager to assert his importance, to tell of his experiences. The respect he desires he has earned: He has done much good work for the church. But he also took part in the darkest scandal in American church history.

I approached him as he was leaving. I told him I had been tough on him in the pages of the *Wall Street Journal*, but that I could see he was a man of depth and talent, and I hoped to speak to him more. His eyes were cold, the kind of cold all writers know when they meet up with someone they've criticized in print. And I had said John Paul should take the cardinal's hat right off his head and find a new cardinal for Boston.

He asked me if it was true that I had said the cardinals of the church should give up their mansions. Yes, I said, I wrote that in the *Journal.*

"Well, we don't need friends of the church turning on the church at such a difficult time," he said. "We need loyalty when the church is going through a tough time, and I don't live in a mansion; you've probably never seen it."

"Yes, I have," I said. "I was in the cardinal's mansion when Cardinal Medeiros was there." I had interviewed Law's predecessor.

Cardinal Law then changed tack. "Well, the cardinal only lives in a modest room, and there have to be conference rooms, and how would it look if I'd refused to live there, what would it say about my predecessor, how would it look?"

How would it look? It would look good. But more to the point, they should not be worrying about how things look; they should be worrying about how things *are*.

I told him that whatever the church did, it was likely to lose the cardinals' residences to trial lawyers, so why not sell them now and put the money in the schools? That caught his attention. I added I would like to talk to him longer some day, have a longer conversation than possible at the moment. He left, angry I think.

He was defensive. They are *all* defensive, the American cardinals. They do not want criticism from their foes and they do not want it from their friends, and they move against those who criticize. And they are like this because they do not understand.

They do not understand what a mother and father go through when their son is sexually violated, how it scars the child, steals his soul, breaks his heart. They try to understand, but they fail. They don't even seem to understand how the scandals happened in the first place. When the first priest violated the first child and no one threw him out, that's how it started.

When I saw them all, the bishops and the cardinals of the church, marching in their miters in procession, in full ceremonial garb, and at receptions and buffets, they seemed to me, by and large, sleek, pink-cheeked, and political. They seemed like career politicians trying to survive in a hard world. Thinking all this was, for me, disorienting and painful. I had always admired the leaders of the American church. I always thought they prayed a lot and were holy. Isn't that their job?

At one point during the beatification Mass, a huge rug bearing the likeness of Mother Teresa smiling joyously was unrolled with a heavy sound from the front of

St. Peter's. It was huge. When it unfurled, the square rang with applause and cheers. And all of the cardinals looked up at her, at this picture of this humble woman, this nobody-saint, this emptied-out person filled with love and bringing love. And I thought: *Maybe that is why God is lifting her up now, maybe that is why John Paul was so committed to her eventual sainthood. He knows she is the template of success for the future of the church. He knows the church, every bit as much as the people of the world, needs to be told who to emulate.*

I came away from the festivities convinced young priests and nuns are the future of the church. Whatever one feels about the hierarchy, it is those not compromised and broken by the scandal who will save the church. It is those who are not flying high but who are doing the on-the-ground work of Christ in the world.

That's what I thought at the end of the beatification, and also that in this uncertain time and uncertain place, the women of the church will, finally, rise. Not to the priesthood — the best of them do not want to be priests and would not want to stoop to equality — but as mothers of the church, as figures of such respect they dwarf the others around them.

And I left moved more than ever by John Paul, who was trying so hard to steer the broken bark of the church, to reconcile its factions, to speak the truth. The sight of him hurt. He spent each day offering his suffering to configure himself more closely to Christ on the cross. And yet at his twenty-fifth anniversary Mass, when they pushed him out in the wheeled throne down the great steps of St. Peter's on a big wooden ramp, with his head at a 45-degree angle, wearing the gold and white miter, the Cardinals arrayed behind him and his handlers smiling at the crowd, I would think, *Oh, I hope it will not be long before he is removed from this cross.* He looked over at us at our last audience, as the American delegation sat in a row of chairs before him. I put my fingers to my lips and turned them toward him. He looked toward us and looked down. And I looked at everyone around me — Kate O'Beirne, Mary Ellen Bork, Mary Ann Glendon — and they had tears in their eyes, because they knew it was good-bye.

CHAPTER FIFTEEN

There Is a Saint Dead in Rome

There is the story of Saint Benedict Joseph Labre, an obscure beggar of eighteenth-century Rome who lived among the poorest of the poor. He wasn't very good at begging. When someone would give him a penny, he'd give it to the beggar nearby. He walked the streets in an old cloak tied at the waist with rope and a sack containing only a Bible and a prayer book slung over his shoulder. He lived to pray, and to receive the sacraments. He walked along and slept in churches. He didn't want anyone to know of or admire his sanctity; he wanted to suffer each day with Christ, wanted to bury his head against Christ's cloak and be unknown, uncelebrated.

The day he died, at age thirty-five, of the old age of the streets, a remarkable thing happened.

As the parish priest who was Benedict's confessor and his only friend wrote, "Scarcely had this poor follower of Christ breathed his last when all at once the little children from the houses hard by filled the whole street with their noise, crying out with one accord: 'The Saint is dead, the Saint is dead.' But [soon] after they were not only young children who published the sanctity of Benedict; all Rome soon joined in their cries, repeating the self-same words: 'A Saint is dead.'. . . Great numbers of persons who have been eminent for their holiness and famous for their miracles have ended the days of their mortal life in this city; but the death of none of them ever excited so rapid and lively an emotion in the midst of the people as the death of this poor beggar. This stirred a kind of universal commotion; for in the streets scarcely anything could be heard but these few words: 'There is a saint dead in Rome. Where is the house in which he has died?' "

Sometimes people know before they're told; sometimes they tell the church before it knows.

I thought of St. Benedict Joseph Labre when John Paul died, and when the world engulfed Rome and people filling the streets began declaring his sainthood. John Paul was no obscure beggar; he had been dying before the cameras of the world for a long time, and so many people had already

— so they thought — said good-bye. But then Europe took to the streets at word of his death, and the four million came and would not be held back. Even when Rome, the day before the funeral, sent out an alarm asking people to stop coming, they would not stop. The city was overwhelmed. The children who took to the streets when St. Benedict died alerted the church to the fact that someone extraordinary had passed; so the millions who went to Rome for John Paul told the church: *He is our hero. He won our hearts. You need to know.*

We live in a time of greatness. It is all around us. There are people whose daily and unknown bravery and kindness must set off fireworks in heaven, and yet among us it is hardly noticed. There is the person who sees that all the opinion of the powerful people in the world is going in one direction, and yet his thoughts and convictions lead him in another, and he summons the courage to follow his convictions, and to take the blows, seen and unseen, that such a decision entails. There are people who find a five-year-old throwaway child in Mexico and bring her up with love in their home, and are grateful in the day to day.

What courage is around us. And the most obvious example was the old man of the Vatican whose crozier shook as he held it high, and whose message was never more eloquent than when he could not speak.

What a death he had. To die in public, with the whole world watching, to work to the very end, to attempt to speak to the world through the window of his Vatican apartments a few days before he died, to struggle and fail and try again, and then to wave, as if he knew we understood. He held on to life as if to show us what he had for so long told us — life is precious, love it, use it, pour yourself out. Spend yourself.

The day after he died, the Sunday *New York Times* reported that John Paul had urged those who loved him not to be sad, and had dictated to his secretary these words: "I am happy, and you should be happy too. Do not weep. Let us pray together with joy."

Soon Father Jarek Cielecki, director of the Vatican Service News, described John Paul's last moments. "The Holy Father died looking towards the window as he prayed, and that shows that in some way he was conscious." Father Cielecki said that just before dying, the pope "raises his right hand in a clear, although simply hinted at, gesture of blessing, as if he became aware of the crowd of faithful present in St. Peter's Square, who in those moments were following the reciting of the Rosary." When the prayer ended, said Father Cielecki, the pope made "a huge effort" and then said the word, "Amen." A moment later he was dead.

And so it turns out that at the last moment of his life, in 2005, the last sound John Paul heard was the saying of prayers on the square below, just as at the moment he was born, in 1920, the first sound the infant Karol Wojtyla heard was the singing of prayers in the church next door.

And there were the mystical suggestions, the whiff of the supernatural in his death. You remember that Saint Malachi, the medieval priest who prophesied future popes, gave a nickname to each. The pope who would be John Paul was denoted with the words *de labore solis* — "of the labors of the sun." On John Paul's birth date, there was a partial solar eclipse. On the day he was buried, there was a partial solar eclipse. In the medieval era a solar eclipse was called the labor of the sun.

You remember the Polish nun, Faustina, who said she was told by Christ that if the

Polish people continued to follow his word, he would bring "a spark out of Poland" who would prepare the world for his second coming. John Paul died on the vigil of the Feast of St. Faustina, after a Mass for the Divine Mercy, of which she spoke, was celebrated in his room. The church duly entered nine days of official mourning. The last day turned out to be the Feast of St. Stanislas, patron saint of Poland. We later learned John Paul had thought to be the first Pope Stanislas, to take that name, and then thought better of it. John Paul it would be.

Great men lift us up. They tell us by their presence that everything is possible, that as children of God we are part of God, and as part of God we can, with him, accomplish anything. *Anything.*

He was an obscure Polish boy with no connections, no standing, without even, by the time he was of college age, a family. He worked in a factory and ate potatoes in water for dinner during a war. He went on to become the most famous man of his age, and famous for that finest of reasons: a life well lived.

And what did he leave behind? He had no possessions. He said in his will that he left behind only notes, which he asked be burned. (His secretary said he would, and then he didn't; history needs them, he said.) He had no family to whom to leave anything if he'd had anything to leave. He mentioned only two people by name in his will: the monsignor who'd been by his side almost every day for forty years, the one who refused to burn the notes, and the former chief rabbi of Rome, who had welcomed John Paul to the Great Synagogue of Rome at the beginning of his pontificate, and become his friend.

When word came that he was gone, I did not feel sad so much as grave. I was in Leesburg, Virginia, for the wedding of a friend. I was about to leave the hotel room when I put on the television to see how he was. He was sick again, and this time it seemed his final illness because he didn't go to the hospital. Popes die in their beds. On NBC, Brian Williams was talking, live, and by the tone of his voice I knew immediately that John Paul was gone. And then: "If you have not already heard or are just tuning in, the news today is the passing of Pope John Paul the Second." I felt a kind of gravity, as if I were experiencing the earth's pull in a conscious way. I sat down and felt grateful for the kindness God had shown in giving him to us.

At the wedding that night, a joyous affair uniting a Christian man with a Muslim woman in a service officiated by a rabbi, everyone talked of the extraordinary ecumenical nature of the ceremony we had just witnessed. There had been groups at the wedding who were wary of one another. They wound up dancing together. A young Orthodox Jewish woman, a stranger to me, came over, took my hand, and said, "I just heard, and I'm so sorry. He was a great man." Beautiful words by which to mark the end of the most embracing of popes, the most embracing of lives.

The next day, on the plane home from Virginia, the shuttle encountered turbulence. I looked down at the thick clouds and the brilliant blue sky above them. I wondered what it was like when John Paul strode into heaven, again able to stride. I wondered if Jesus was standing there, putting out his arms, and if John Paul had gone to him and put his head upon Christ's breast. I wondered if John Paul at that moment had turned into a child, a baby, and was held in Christ's arms. I wondered what perfect happiness feels like. I wondered if those you love who are already up there come forward with radiant smiles. I once met a hospice nurse, a working-class Jewish girl in New Jersey, whose job it was, essentially, to help people die. I asked her what she had found out from her work that she hadn't known when she began it. She said, "Nobody dies alone." I wasn't sure what she meant. "Nobody dies alone. Something happens at the end. Someone comes and helps them over. Their eyes open, and they say a name or make a gesture. Somebody helps them."

Then I thought, as I mused on the plane, John Paul at this moment is probably dressed in white robes and he's young and healthy, forty, a man at the height of his powers, and his face isn't frozen anymore, and he can show joy.

These thoughts seem sentimental, but I do not mean them so. I have become a person who believes these things.

The next morning on *Good Morning America*, Diane Sawyer did a report saying that 77 percent of Americans believed in a literal heaven. I was there in the studio and before the piece ran, a beautiful young producer told me she had had a surprising experience. She had been brought up as a child in the Philippines and her family had always been Catholic. Then some of them had become evangelical Protestants, and they began taking her to their new church. That didn't feel right to her, not that she was that interested, and she fell away from practice and belief. Now it's years later and the pope has died and she finds herself sobbing. She didn't know why. She called her old aunt, the one who had stayed Catholic. The old aunt would be terribly sad, and they could weep together. But the old aunt was serene. John Paul was old and suffering, she said, and now he was happy, with his Father. Don't be sad, it is all as it should be.

I asked the producer what she did then. She said she thought about her sobs and her aunt's serenity, and what that might imply.

People think more about their souls than they say. They think more about their souls than they know.

For the piece with Diane, I'd brought a prayer card given out at the funeral five years earlier of a mutual friend, Nick Forstmann. He had died in young middle age of cancer, and his death had been a sharp blow to all who knew him. At his funeral, the card they gave out had on the front of it a picture I had never seen. Most Catholic funeral cards bear images of saints or the Holy Mother, and the art is old-fashioned and traditional. But that is changing, I think in part because the Protestant evangelical style of seeing Christ as a person who is your friend has slowly but surely reentered the Catholic church, and happily so. Nick's Mass card was a drawing of a man being received by Christ in heaven. Christ is hugging him in a big bear hug, as if to say, "Welcome home, my brother." That is how the Forstmanns saw Nick in the days after his death. I showed Diane the card and said, "This is how a lot of people see what is happening now to John Paul." She kept the card on the table beside her throughout the interview. Later I would give her a poster of the newest version of this card: a painting of the Virgin Mary hugging and welcoming John Paul.

One of the most remarkable things about the days after the death of the pope was that everyone was interested, everyone cared, no matter what his or her beliefs or lack of belief. My friend Dan, an Episcopalian who always describes himself as not much of a Christian, found as he watched the coverage of the pope's decline that he was identifying with him. He didn't know why, but he felt a strong spiritual connection. He kind of loved him, he said, which left him perplexed. I said, "Maybe the Holy Spirit within you jumps when it sees the Holy Spirit within him." As we discussed this possibility, I realized that I now feel no more self-conscious saying "the Holy Spirit within you" than a child feels saying, "That's a tree."

That is a gift. It had not been mine until John Paul walked into my life and served, unknowingly, as my spiritual father. He had led me like a light in the dark, like Jim Caviezel's small lit match in a big dark factory.

The funeral itself may have been the greatest evangelical event since Gutenberg printed the Bible.

It was a phenomenon, certainly the biggest funeral in all human history, not only the four million who filled the streets, but the two to three *billion* people estimated to have watched or seen it on television. Two to three billion listened to the readings, experienced the Mass, and so it was the biggest Mass in human history. Two to three billion heard the eulogy. A few days later, my friend Laura Ingraham, a convert to Catholicism, said at lunch, "You watch, the next story is going to be millions of conversions. That was his last gift to all of us."

And what of the effect on the leaders of the world? Presidents, princes, patriarchs, kings; the new leader of a war-torn democracy sitting here, the angry ayatollahs of a yearning nation there, the Dalai Lama, dictators. They were all there, at St. Peter's, witnessing, watching, hearing.

And throughout the world those who could not come held, at the moment of the funeral, public Masses — in Washington, in Beijing, in Mexico City. They held a Mass in the Blonie Field, in Kraków. A network went there, live. Again a million came, but this time they did not chant "We want God!" This time they wept.

But there was something else about the funeral. During it, during the coverage, the whole world seemed to stop. It became still. Did you notice? As if time were suspended, as if the Western world, the whole world of ambition and industry and calculation and material thoughts — stopped.

And something startling: The silence was loud. You could stop whatever you were doing and look up, and what you saw on the television was the wind silently turning the pages of the open Bible that was on top of John Paul's casket in the middle of the square, as they said the Mass around him, and you started as if you had heard something loud.

And let me tell you when the whole world began again. It was when the vast crowd burst into cheers and tears and shouts and applause as Cardinal Joseph Ratzinger spoke, in his eulogy, of who John Paul really was.

This was amazing, what the crowds did. Because *the people took over.* Catholics at Mass, certainly a funeral Mass, are quiet and observant, but here they were saying, *We are not observers! We are part of this — we have a voice now, hear us.*

And you could see from the crowd that it was everybody, all ages and countries. *The whole church was there.*

And as Cardinal Ratzinger spoke, the crowd stepped in and took part, and he looked out at them and he stopped, and he let them speak. He did not try to quiet them. He listened. He seemed almost to be encouraging them. The sound they made filled Rome.

But also, the world was looking in a new

way at Cardinal Ratzinger, the main cele-
brator of the Mass and eulogist of John
Paul. Who had chosen him for that role?
John Paul. Who had brought the crowds to
Rome? John Paul. And now all the crowds,
all the world, were looking at Ratzinger,
who was too old and controversial to be a
pope, everyone knew, and yet . . .

His eulogy was amazingly personal. He
spoke of who John Paul really was, and
what his life really meant:

"Follow me." The Risen Lord says these
words to Peter. They are his last words to
this disciple, chosen to shepherd his flock.
"Follow me." This . . . saying of Christ
can be taken as the key to understanding
the message which comes to us from the
life of our late beloved Pope John Paul II.
Today we bury his remains in the earth as
a seed of immortality — our hearts are
full of sadness, yet at the same time of
joyful hope and profound gratitude. . . .

"Follow me." As a young student Karol
Wojtyla was thrilled by literature, the
theatre, and poetry. Working in a chemical plant, surrounded and threatened by
the Nazi terror, he heard the voice of the
Lord: Follow me! In this extraordinary
setting he began to read books of philos-

ophy and theology, and then entered the clandestine seminary established by Cardinal Sapieha. . . .

How often, in his letters to priests and in his autobiographical books, has he spoken to us about his priesthood, to which he was ordained on 1 November 1946. In these texts he interprets his priesthood with particular reference to three sayings of the Lord. First: "You did not choose me, but I chose you. And I appointed you to go and bear fruit, fruit that will last." (John 15:16). The second saying is: "The good shepherd lays down his life for the sheep." (John 10:11). And then: "As the Father has loved me, so I have loved you; abide in my love." (John 15:9). In these three sayings we see the heart and soul of our Holy Father.

He really went everywhere, untiringly, in order to bear fruit, fruit that lasts. *Rise, Let Us Be on Our Way!* is the title of his next-to-last book. "Rise, let us be on our way!" With these words he roused us from a lethargic faith, from the sleep of the disciples of both yesterday and today. "Rise, let us be on our way!" he continues to say to us even today.

The Holy Father was a priest to the last, for he offered his life to God for his flock and for the entire human family, in a daily self-oblation for the service of the Church, especially amid the sufferings of his final months. And in this way he became one with Christ, the Good Shepherd who loves his sheep. . . .

"Follow me!" In July 1958 the young priest Karol Wojtyla began a new stage in his journey with the Lord and in the footsteps of the Lord. Karol had gone . . . for his usual vacation, along with a group of young people who loved canoeing. But he brought with him a letter inviting him to call on the Primate of Poland, Cardinal Wyszynski. He could guess the purpose of the meeting: he was to be appointed as the auxiliary Bishop of Kraków. Leaving the academic world, leaving this challenging engagement with young people, leaving the great intellectual endeavour of striving to understand and interpret the mystery of that creature which is man and of communicating to today's world the Christian interpretation of our being — all this must have seemed to him like losing his very self, losing what had become the very human identity of this young priest.

"Follow me." Karol Wojtyla accepted the appointment, for he heard in the

Church's call the voice of Christ. And then he realized how true are the Lord's words: "Those who try to make their life secure will lose it, but those who lose their life will keep it." (Luke 17:33).

Our Pope — and we all know this — never wanted to make his own life secure, to keep it for himself; he wanted to give of himself unreservedly, to the very last moment, for Christ and thus also for us. And thus he came to experience how everything which he had given over into the Lord's hands came back to him in a new way. His love of words, of poetry, of literature, became an essential part of his pastoral mission and gave new vitality, new urgency, new attractiveness to the preaching of the Gospel. . . .

"Follow me!" In October 1978 Cardinal Wojtyla once again heard the voice of the Lord. Once more there took place that dialogue with Peter reported in the Gospel of this Mass: "Simon, son of John, do you love me? Feed my sheep!" To the Lord's question, "Karol, do you love me?," the Archbishop of Kraków answered from the depths of his heart: "Lord you know everything; you know that I love you." The love of Christ was the dominant force in the life of our beloved Holy Father. Anyone who ever saw him pray, who ever heard him preach, knows that. Thanks to his being profoundly rooted in Christ, he was able to bear a burden which transcends merely human abilities: that of being the shepherd of Christ's flock, his universal Church. . . .

I would like only to read two passages of today's liturgy which reflect central elements of his message. In the first reading, Saint Peter says — and with Saint Peter, the Pope himself — "I truly understand that God shows no partiality, but in every nation anyone who fears him and does what is right is acceptable to him. You know the message he sent to the people of Israel, preaching peace by Jesus Christ — he is Lord of all." And in the second reading, Saint Paul — and with Saint Paul, our late Pope — exhorts us, crying out: "My brothers and sisters, whom I love and long for, my joy and my crown, stand firm in the Lord in this way, my beloved."

"Follow me!" Together with the command to feed his flock, Christ proclaimed to Peter that he would die a martyr's death. With those words, which conclude and sum up the dialogue on love and on the mandate of the universal shepherd, the Lord recalls another dialogue, which took place during the Last Supper. There Jesus had said: "Where I am going, you cannot come." Peter said to him, "Lord, where are you going?" Jesus replied: "Where I am going, you cannot follow me now; but you will follow me afterward." Jesus from the Supper went towards the Cross, went towards his resurrection — he entered into the paschal mystery; and Peter could not yet follow him. Now — after the resurrection — comes the time, comes this "afterward." By shepherding the flock of Christ, Peter enters into the paschal mystery, he goes towards the cross and the resurrection. The Lord says this in these words: ". . . when you were younger, you used to fasten your own belt and to go wherever you wished. But when you grow old, you will stretch out your hands, and someone else will fasten a belt around you and take you where you do not wish to go." In the first years of his pontificate, still young and full of energy, the Holy Father went to the very ends of the earth, guided by Christ. But afterwards, he increasingly entered into the communion of Christ's sufferings; increasingly he understood the truth of the words: "Someone else will fasten a belt around you." And in this very communion with the suffering Lord, tirelessly and with renewed intensity, he proclaimed the Gospel, the mystery of that love which goes to the end.

He interpreted for us the paschal mystery as a mystery of divine mercy. In his last book, he wrote: "The limit imposed upon evil 'is ultimately Divine Mercy' " (*Memory and Identity*, pages 60–61).

And reflecting on the assassination attempt, he said: "In sacrificing himself for us all, Christ gave a new meaning to suffering, opening up a new dimension, a new order: the order of love. . . . It is this suffering which burns and consumes evil with the flame of love and draws forth even from sin a great flowering of good." Impelled by this vision, the Pope suffered and loved in communion with Christ, and that is why the message of his suffering and his silence proved so eloquent and so fruitful. . . .

[T]he Holy Father found the purest reflection of God's mercy in the Mother of God. He, who at an early age had lost his own mother, loved his divine mother all the more. He heard the words of the crucified Lord as addressed personally to him: "Behold your Mother." And so he did as the beloved disciple did: he took her into his own home — *Totus tuus.* And from the mother he learned to conform himself to Christ.

None of us can ever forget how in that last Easter Sunday of his life, the Holy Father, marked by suffering, came once more to the window of the Apostolic Palace and one last time gave his blessing. . . .

We can be sure that our beloved Pope is standing today at the window of the Father's house, that he sees us and blesses us. Yes, bless us, Holy Father. We entrust your dear soul to the Mother of God, your Mother, who guided you each day and who will guide you now to the eternal glory of her Son, our Lord Jesus Christ. Amen.

I was at home, working, and watching it all on TV. I was fascinated, moved. I'd been stunned by Cardinal Ratzinger's eulogy as I listened to the translation, and for the first time found myself thinking: Maybe he is the one. I would be so happy with his choice, with his election. I sent an e-mail to a friend at National Review Online. It said, "Ratzinger may — may — just have made himself pope this morning." She told me I was being too optimistic. I knew she was probably right. And yet . . .

I had not paid deep attention to Ratzinger the past few years. I knew he was brave and serious, was John Paul's close friend, knew he saw doctrine and theology as John Paul did; I knew he loved the church and tried in his own way to protect, correct, and advance it. But he was old, controversial, and German. In fact, he was considered to be too old and controversial for the papacy a decade ago. He had tried twice to retire.

I'd been deeply impressed by print reports of his declaration to the cardinals before the voting had begun. The world we live in is being swept by a "dictatorship of relativism," a growing inability to see and state truth. The old church was taking on water from all sides. Implicit in his statement: We need a great and truthful captain. But that very speech seemed to me to be the cardinal's way of saying it wouldn't be him. A real contender would not have been so sharp, would not have declared his thinking so clearly. And Ratzinger had spoken just weeks before, during Easter week, when John Paul was still alive, of the "filth" that had entered the church. Would the cardinals vote for a man who they thought would take a great broom to the stables? That would be . . . surprising. Later I would read a report in *La Stampa* of a chance meeting between a retired curial monsignor and Cardinal Ratzinger, two days after Ratzinger had shared his Easter reflections. The monsignor asked the cardinal why he had given such a discouraging picture of the church. Ratzinger, according to *La Stampa*, had told the monsignor, "You weren't born yesterday, you understand what I'm talking about, you know what it means. We priests! We priests!" The monsignor said the cardinal spoke in a pleading tone. Struck by this, and by Ratzinger's request that he pray to the Sacred Heart to ask for the pardon of the sins of priests, the monsignor did not press him further.

It was heartening and even inspiring to think this important cardinal understood what is happening in our church.

I was up at 4:00 a.m. to watch the cardinals enter the Sistine Chapel for the first day of voting. I followed the voting. I saw the dark smoke. And then that afternoon, late in the afternoon, 5:50 p.m. Rome time on April 19th, an amazing thing: the white smoke. It looked white, it seemed white, it did not turn dark. But the Vatican had promised to ring its great bell if a pope had been chosen, and bells were not ringing. However, the crowd in the square seemed to know what the anchormen didn't. Everyone was reporting live from Rome, and the reporters had to keep saying, "We do not believe that is white smoke, but the crowd certainly does." The crowd was cheering and applauding and would not leave the square.

Once again the people were ahead of everyone else.

And then the great bell began to ring.

And, oh, what happened then. Did you see it? The networks were doing big broad shots of St. Peter's and its environs, and suddenly you could see them running. The bell was ringing, and they came running in from the offices and streets of Rome, running in their business suits, in jeans with backpacks over their shoulders. So many came running that by the end, by the time the new pope was announced, St. Peter's and the streets leading to it were as full as they'd been two weeks ago, at the funeral of John Paul II.

It was amazing to see, and the networks showed it for almost an hour as the world waited to see who would come out on the balcony.

No advance word. No one knew who it was. All they knew was that against expectations he had been elected quickly, on the fourth vote.

Then, movement on the balcony. The curtains behind the glass doors moved. They moved again, and then the doors opened. It was 6:43 p.m., early dusk, not dark yet.

Out marched a bevy of cardinals and assistants. The one standing in front, Cardinal Jorge Arturo Medina Estevez of Chile, began to speak.

"I announce to you a great joy; we have a pope."

He paused. Later Cardinal Estevez would say he did it deliberately, as if to draw out the good news.

"Eminentissimum ac Reverendissimum Dominum, Dominum Josephum —"

At this point I shook my head. Josephum? Cardinal Ratzinger's first name is Joseph.

"Sanctae Romanae Ecclesiae Cardinalem Ratzinger qui sibi nomen imposuit Benedictum XVI."

"The most eminent and reverend Cardinal Ratzinger, who has taken the name Benedict XVI."

And now he walked out onto the balcony, and raised his hands, and the crowd yelled "Papa!" and "Benedict!" Cardinal Joseph Ratzinger of Germany was supreme pontiff, successor of Peter, the man who would follow John Paul. He spoke briefly. He called himself a poor servant. He lauded Mary.

He is old, with rings under his eyes like an owl's, he is tall with thick white hair, he is sweet and courtly, but unlike John Paul — you can see it — he is shy.

I thought two things.

One was that those pursuing the cause of John Paul's canonization need look no further for his first miracle: It is Benedict XVI.

And I thought that John Paul had bestowed upon his old friend Benedict a gift of inestimable value: He had left a flock in the habit of loving a pope. And they would now transfer that love to Benedict.

It was all so beautiful and so . . . confusing. The one man the cardinals could depend on to attempt to clean up the church had been elected — almost unanimously! — by the cardinals who, many of them, had taken actions that had left it tarnished. I didn't understand. Two great men in a row. That isn't what history does; history doesn't give you two Lincolns one after another. Later, a reporter who is a friend and who was there in Rome for a Catholic media organization, a man who knows pretty much everyone in the Vatican, told me he knew the answer. Everyone who didn't want Ratzinger was disorganized; they never got together, never got behind a candidate.

Disorganized? How could that be? The liberals of the church, as they are called, the left, had been waiting a decade for John Paul to die. They had plenty of time to organize.

"They didn't have a candidate," he said. Some tried to build support for Cardinal Martini, a brilliant man and considered a liberal, but the cardinals soon concluded they already had a leader — "and it was Ratzinger."

A month after the conclave, this testimony came from a cardinal who had chatted with warmth and a certain lack of discretion to a group of Catholics on the Internet. His remarks were reported by the news organization Zenit. The retired archbishop of Barcelona, seventy-eight-year-old Cardinal Ricard Maria Carles, said that in the general congregation, at the beginning of the conclave, each cardinal was given seven minutes to address the congregation, to express his views on "the world and the Church" but not speak of the profile of a potential new pope. They spoke rather of local problems, local joys and challenges. "To experience this," he said, "was a grace from God." All of the cardinals, he said, "were conscious that these 115 men had to choose, with the Holy Spirit, the one who would govern" more than a billion Catholics. Every time they voted, "with our vote in hand, when going up to the altar, and seeing the Christ of the Last Judgment surrounded by the Sistine Chapel . . . we said the formula, 'I swear before this Christ, who will judge me!'" He said, "When one is there, there is no place for 'lobbies,' or pressure groups, or the like, or any of that!" Then he explained how the voting went as it did: "What you see, when 115 persons of different races and cultures are in agreement on the fourth ballot, what you see is that the Holy Spirit acts. One did not vote for someone one liked, or of a similar culture: It was the Spirit."

When two thirds of the vote, the minimum needed for election, went for Cardinal Ratzinger, there was applause. Then the tallying continued, and when it was over, Cardinal Carles saw a German cardinal, Cardinal Meisner of Cologne, "a very, very serious man, crying like a child . . . overwhelmed."

Soon the nuns and service staff met with the new Holy Father. They kissed him on the hand, and he kissed them on the cheek. "And pictures were taken kissing the Pope!" said Cardinal Carles. "This is the one they call 'the great inquisitor.' "

Cardinal Carles's explanation — that the Holy Spirit did it — seems to me the best and only explanation.

But here is another question to take from the events of Rome in 2005, from the death of one pope and the elevation of another. And it may be an even bigger one: Why did they run? Why was Rome engulfed? Why did such ancient news — the pope is dead; we have a pope — representing such irrelevant-seeming truths and such an archaic institution — make them run? Why did they gather, what did they have to hear?

The faith is dead in Europe; we all know that. And yet they came running. Some must have wanted just to witness history, wanted to be there and click pictures with their cell phones. But not all, not most. We know this from their unfeigned and even passionate sadness, and then joy. We saw them weep as the new pope came out. We heard them chant his new name. Why were they jubilant?

People are complicated. You can hit distracted people with all the propaganda in the world; you can give it to them every day in all your media, and sometimes they'll tell pollsters they agree with you. But something is always going on in their chests. Some truth is known there; some yearning lives there. It's as if they have a compass in their hearts and turn as they will, this way and that, it continues to point to true north.

And this: We all want a spiritual father. Whatever the circumstances of your life or family, whatever strong fathers you have in your life, we all want a spiritual father. We want someone who will stand for what is difficult and right, what is impossible but true. We are human, and so we don't always want to live by the truth or be governed by it. But we are grateful when someone *stands* for it. And when he walks onto the balcony and you can see him and reach to him and know he is there — well, that is something.

And so in the weeks that followed these events, this is how I felt: It is all right that John Paul is dead, he is with his father, at the window. And now we have a new Holy Father, and he is brave and serious. He will lead us through some amount of tumult. The church, especially in America, will be swept by clamor, by tugs and pushes of left and right and modernists and traditionalists and lovers of the faith and players with the faith. We continue in interesting times.

And with what attitude should we move forward? "Be not afraid." Those famous words of John Paul, the words he used for a quarter century. And now the new pope said them on the second day of his pontificate. He said, "Be not afraid," and I thought, Good, this is a man who knows what time it is. And so he became for me, at that moment, Big Ben.

BIBLIOGRAPHY

Bernstein, Carl, and Marco Politi. *His Holiness: John Paul II and the History of Our Time.* New York: Doubleday, 1996.

Cambridge Center for the Study of Faith and Culture. *The Pope Speaks to the American Church: John Paul II's Homilies, Speeches, and Letters to Catholics in the United States.* Foreword by Cardinal Bernard Law. New York: HarperCollins, 1992.

Dulles, Avery. *The Splendor of Faith: The Theological Vision of Pope John Paul II.* New York: Herder & Herder, 1999.

Encyclicals of John Paul II, The. Edited with Introductions by J. Michael Miller, C.S.B. Huntington, IN: Our Sunday Visitor Publishing Division, 1996.

Flynn, Ray, with Robin Moore and Jim Vrabel, *John Paul II: A Personal Portrait of the Pope and the Man.* New York: St. Martin's Press, 2001.

Goodier, Alban, S.J. *Saints for Sinners.* San Francisco: Ignatius Press, 1993.

John Paul II, Pope. *The Splendor of Truth, Veritatis Splendor,* Vatican translation. Boston: Pauline Books & Media, undated.

——. *The Theology of the Body: Human Love in the Divine Plan.* Foreword by John S. Grabowski, Ph.D. Boston: Pauline Books & Media, 1997.

——. *Rise, Let Us Be on Our Way.* Walter Ziemba, tr. New York: Warner Books, 2004.

Kwitney, Jonathan. *Man of the Century: The Life and Times of Pope John Paul II.* New York: Henry Holt and Company, Inc., 1997.

Melady, Margaret B. *The Rhetoric of Pope John Paul II.* Westport, CT: Praeger, 1999.

O'Brien, Darcy. *The Hidden Pope.* New York: Daybreak Books, 1998.

Pope in America, The. Brian C. Anderson, ed. Introduced by Michael Novak. South Bend, IN: Crisis Books, 1996.

Svidercoschi, Gian Franco. *Stories of Karol: The Unknown Life of John Paul II.* Peter Heinegg, tr. Liguori, MO: Liguori/Triumph, 2003.

Szostak, John M., with Frances Spatz

Leighton. *In the Footsteps of Pope John Paul II.* Englewood Cliffs, NJ: Prentice-Hall, 1980.

Szulc, Tad. *Pope John Paul II.* New York: Scribner, 1995.

Weigel, George. *Witness to Hope.* New York: HarperCollins, 1999.

Wojtyla, Karol. *Love and Responsibility.* San Francisco: Ignatius Press, 1993.